CONTENTS

INTRODUCTION – THE EXAMINATION

Before you can receive a course award in Higher History, you must pass the three internal units, which are assessed by your teacher or lecturer, and also the external examination.

The course you are studying is taken from one of three options:

◆ **Option A – Medieval History**

◆ **Option B – Early Modern History**

◆ **Option C – Later Modern History**

Each of these options is divided into three units, like this:

	Medieval	Early Modern	Later Modern
Historical Study: Scottish and British	Medieval Society	Scotland in the Age of the Reformation (1542–1603) **Or** Scotland and England in the Century of Revolutions (1603–1702)	Britain 1850s–1979
Historical Study: European and World	Nation and King **Or** Crisis of Authority	Royal Authority in 17th and 18th Century Europe **Or** The French Revolution: The Emergence of the Citizen State	The Growth of Nationalism (Germany **or** Italy) **Or** The Large Scale State (The USA **or** Russia)
Historical Special Topic	Norman Conquest and Expansion (1050–1153) **Or** The Crusades (1096–1204)	Scotland 1689–1715 **Or** The Atlantic Slave Trade **Or** The American Revolution	Patterns of Migration: Scotland 1830s–1930s **Or** Appeasement and the Road to War, to 1939 **Or** The Origins and Development of the Cold War (1945–1985) **Or** Ireland 1900–1985: A Divided Identity

The examination is divided into three parts. There are two unseen papers, usually taken in May, and there is an Extended Essay, for which you write your own question, have some time to carry out research and create a plan. You then use the plan to guide your writing during the writing-up session, when you have two hours under examination conditions to complete your essay.

Paper 1 tests the first two units (Historical Study: Scottish and British and Historical Study: European and World). For each unit you must write one essay in the examination. In the Scottish and British unit you may choose one from five questions, and in the European and World unit, one from four.

Paper 2 tests your ability to work with sources within your Historical Special Topic. In this paper you must use the five sources provided as well as your recalled knowledge to answer all five questions in the Special Topic you are studying.

This book will consider all three parts of the examination, and offer advice to help you master the skills you need in each one. In the section dealing with essay writing, and especially in the Tasks, examples are offered from all parts of the syllabus – Medieval, Early Modern and Later Modern, though more frequently from the more commonly studied areas.

In discussing approaches to source-handling questions, it would be too complex and probably confusing to give examples from all areas of study. As a result most, though not all, examples are taken from the most commonly studied Historical Special Topic – Appeasement and the Road to War. However, the skills discussed and methods of answering the questions apply equally to all Historical Special Topics, and in devising the Tasks I have tried either to make them independent of the period of study or to supply at least some examples in less common areas. Many sources in the examination have been edited to assist candidates. When I have used sources that have appeared in past papers I have used these edited versions to avoid confusion.

Hints and Tips

If you prepare carefully, learning the skills as well as the factual knowledge needed to help you demonstrate them properly, you can face the examination with confidence. It is important to understand that the examiners are not trying to catch you out. They try to set questions that will allow you to show what you can do and what you have learned, not to trick you in some way. Likewise, markers are encouraged to reward good work, not to look for mistakes as an excuse to take marks off.

Being prepared

It is a good feeling to enter an examination room feeling prepared. There are two parts to this. One is developing your skills in writing essays and handling sources, and that is what most of this book is about. The other part is just as important. To make the most of the skills you need to do the memory part, learning the facts that you need to show understanding of the historical events and issues. There is no shortcut to this. No matter how able you are, this bit depends on determination and hard work.

It may help to plan your work out well in advance – to have a revision diary that allocates certain days and times to revising each of your subjects. That is how I prepared for my Highers, in days before some of the events you may be studying for History even took place! I decided which topics to study, when and for how long. (By the way, be realistic – how long can you spend concentrating on one subject before your brain goes numb?) I split my time into one-hour sessions, usually two per night with a break of 15 minutes between – not more or I'd never have gone back. Each session was on a different subject (e.g. first Maths, then History, or first French, then Chemistry) to make me think in different ways.

The method of study was as important as the time spent. Just reading something over and over leads to your eyes moving over the paper while your brain is thinking of something else altogether, and you learn next to nothing. It is much more effective to write down the points you want to remember, and *not* in the same format as the book or notes from which you are studying. If it is in paragraphs, break it down into lists. Next time, perhaps create a spider diagram. Anything to make you *think* about what you are writing. That way, you remember more. Sometimes I wrote the same stuff down six or eight times, all in different ways. Some of it must have stuck, or I wouldn't be writing this now.

Hints and Tips

It is important not to shut yourself away all the time and just study, because one thing you discover about learning is that the more you learn, the more you realise what you don't know, and that can be frightening. You think it is only happening to you. Discuss your study and your concerns with friends and you will see that they feel the same way. Actually, if you have been studying properly, you have probably learned more than you think, and so have they. To test this, ask someone you really trust to ask you questions about what you have been studying, using your notes. This will reinforce your learning when you get something right; it will also tell you what you need to revise again if you get something wrong.

If you do study in a methodical way, you will feel prepared and confident. In sitting examinations that is more than half the battle.

In the examination room

In both papers, the most important thing is to use your time effectively. This means splitting it in a way that gives you enough time to answer each question as well as you can.

In the essay paper, it is wise to time yourself so that, as nearly as possible, you spend the same time on each of your two answers. You may be tempted to take longer on a question you really know well, but you may leave too little time to write a decent answer for the second question, and may lose more marks there than you gain by spending longer on the first one.

In the source paper, look at the number of marks for each question, and write answers of an appropriate length. It makes no sense to write more for a question worth four marks than for one worth seven or eight. More than once I have marked an answer worth full marks and found there was still a page of writing to read, and that an answer later in the paper for more marks was only a few lines long because the person had run out of time. Markers cannot give more than 4 out of 4 or 5 out of 5, but they *can* give 6 or 7 out of 8! If it helps, you can, of course, answer the questions in any order you like, as long as you write the correct question number against each answer.

Finally ...

Good luck with your examination, though if you have done your preparation you should not really need it!

Ian Matheson

SECTION 1

Essay Questions

Chapter 1

ANSWERING ESSAY QUESTIONS

What do you need to know?

In order to write a good essay, you need to have a good knowledge of the period you are studying. This gives you the evidence you will use to show your essay writing skills at their best. This book cannot be a textbook containing all the information you need to know, but below is an indication of the kinds of information you will need, divided by the options you may be studying. This is not a complete list, but should be a reasonable guide.

Medieval History

Medieval Society in twelfth-century England and Scotland

The feudal system and serfdom	◆ What were the main features of the feudal system? ◆ How important was the feudal system in governing England and Scotland? ◆ What parts did royalty, nobles, knights and serfs have in society, and what were the relationships between them? ◆ How well did the system work?
Towns	◆ Why did towns grow in the twelfth century? ◆ What functions did they have in medieval society? ◆ How important were towns, and especially royal burghs, in medieval society?
The Church	◆ What were the differences between the regular and secular Church? ◆ How important was religion in everyday life? ◆ What different roles did the Church have in medieval society – economic, political and social as well as religious?
Feudal monarchy – the reigns of David I in Scotland and Henry II in England	◆ How far did each of these monarchs strengthen royal power? ◆ In what ways did they change their countries, especially in developing law, order and justice? ◆ What were their relations with the Church?

Nation and King

King John and Magna Carta	◆ What were the reasons for the growth of opposition to King John of England among his barons? ◆ In what ways and with what results did they show their opposition? ◆ What was the importance of Magna Carta?
The reigns of Philip II and Louis IX in France	◆ What were the achievements of each of these kings? ◆ What were the reasons for their success? ◆ Why was there little opposition to these kings from the French barons?
The Scottish Wars of Independence (1286–1328)	◆ Why did a sense of national identity (being Scottish) develop at this time? ◆ Why did the Wars of Independence take place? ◆ What was the idea of the 'Community of the Realm' and why was it important? ◆ How important were William Wallace and Robert Bruce in the Scottish opposition to England? ◆ What were the reasons for eventual Scottish victory?

Crisis of Authority

The Hundred Years' War	◆ Why did the Hundred Years' War take place? ◆ What economic, social and political effects did the war have on France and England? ◆ What were the reasons for early English successes and final French victory?
Social upheaval	◆ What effects did the Black Death have on England, Scotland and continental Europe? ◆ What were the Peasants' Revolt and the Jacquerie? ◆ What effects did they have in changing medieval society?
The Church in crisis (1305–1450)	◆ What were the causes of crisis within the Church during this period? ◆ What were the effects of the Avignon Papacy, Great Schism and Conciliar Movement on the authority of the Church and on medieval society?

Early Modern History

Scotland in the Age of the Reformation (1542–1603)

Scotland in 1542	◆ What was the Scottish political and social structure like in 1542? ◆ What were the weaknesses of the Church in Scotland? ◆ Why did the Church prove unable to reform itself?
Relationships with England and France	◆ What effects did the 'Rough Wooing' have on Scotland's foreign relations? ◆ How important were the effects of relations with England and France on events in Scotland? ◆ Why was the move of Mary Queen of Scots to France important?
The Protestant Reformation	◆ What were the differences between Protestant and Roman Catholic beliefs and ways of worship? ◆ Why did the Protestant Reformation succeed in Scotland? ◆ For what reasons were Roman Catholics persecuted after the Reformation?
Mary Queen of Scots	◆ What problems did Mary face on her return to Scotland? ◆ Why did Mary have difficulties in her relationship with the Scottish nobles? ◆ What were the reasons that caused Mary to lose her throne and her life?
Scotland as a Protestant country	◆ In what ways did Scotland change as a result of the Reformation? ◆ How important was the growth of Presbyterianism to Scottish society and government?
The personal rule of James VI	◆ How successful was James VI in controlling Scotland? ◆ In what ways did the relationship between the Church and the state change between 1542 and 1603?

Scotland and England in the Century of Revolutions (1603–1702)

Britain in 1603	◆ What were the effects of the Union of the Crowns in England and Scotland?
The challenge to royal authority	◆ What religious, political and economic issues led to conflict between kings and parliaments during the reigns of James VI and I and Charles I? ◆ Why did the Covenanter movement grow in Scotland? ◆ Why did problems between king and parliament lead to Civil War?

The Interregnum	◆ What different forms of government were set up between 1649 and 1660? ◆ What problems made it difficult to set up an alternative form of government that would last? ◆ Why did none of the new forms of government survive?
The 'Glorious Revolution'	◆ Why did the 'Glorious Revolution' take place? ◆ What difference did the 'Glorious Revolution' make to the way Britain was governed? ◆ What difference did it make to the lives of the British people?

Royal Authority in seventeenth and eighteenth century Europe

Louis XIV and France	◆ What was the idea of 'absolutism'? ◆ What were the features of the government system of Louis XIV? ◆ How accurate is it to describe his government as 'absolute'? ◆ What were the main problems facing Louis XIV and his ministers? ◆ How successfully did they solve these problems?
Enlightened absolutism in the eighteenth century: case studies of Frederick the Great of Prussia and Joseph II of the Habsburg Empire	◆ What did the idea of 'enlightened absolutism' mean? ◆ Did the rule of Frederick the Great show that he deserved to be called an 'enlightened absolutist'? ◆ Did the rule of Joseph II show that he deserved to be called an 'enlightened absolutist'?
The domestic policies of Frederick the Great and Joseph II	◆ What were the effects of the rule of Frederick the Great on the people of Prussia? ◆ What were the effects of the rule of Joseph II on the people of the Habsburg Empire? ◆ How successful was each in achieving his aims?

The French Revolution: The Emergence of the Citizen State

The Ancien Régime	◆ What were the features of the Ancien Régime? ◆ What were its weaknesses?
The challenge to royal authority in the 1780s	◆ What were the reasons for the growth of unrest among the three Estates in France during the 1780s? ◆ How important were the claims of the nobles, the parlements, the bourgeoisie and the peasants in causing a challenge to royal authority? ◆ What part did the ideas of the Enlightenment have in leading to rebellion?
The Revolution	◆ For what reasons did discontent turn into violent revolution in 1789?

Changing government in France to 1799	◆ What different types of government were tried in France between 1789 and 1799?
	◆ Why did the revolution become increasingly violent between 1792 and 1794?
	◆ Why were there so many changes of government during this period?
	◆ What changes did the revolution and its aftermath make to the lives of the French people?

Later Modern History

Britain 1850s–1979

Democracy and the British people	◆ What are the main features of a democracy?
	◆ What changes took place to make Britain more democratic between 1867 and 1928?
	◆ Did these changes make Britain a democratic country?
	◆ For what reasons did parliament pass the reforms that widened the franchise and extended democracy during this period?
	◆ How far did these changes affect the way Britain is governed?
Political and popular attempts to influence authority	◆ Why did the Labour movement grow in Britain between the 1890s and 1922?
	◆ What did those who founded the movement want it to achieve?
	◆ How successful was the movement in achieving these aims by 1922?
	◆ Why did movements for women's suffrage grow in the late nineteenth and early twentieth centuries?
	◆ In what ways did they try to influence governments to give women the right to vote?
	◆ How successful were their efforts?
	◆ For what reasons did women gain the right to vote by 1928?
Government and people: social problems and social reform	◆ What social problems did Britain face in 1900?
	◆ What changes took place in the attitudes of governments towards social reform between 1900 and 1951?
	◆ What does the idea of a 'Welfare State' mean?
	◆ Why did the Liberal Government of 1906–1914 pass reforms to tackle poverty?
	◆ How big a change did these reforms make to people's lives?
	◆ What effects did the Great Depression have on the British people?
	◆ What did the National Government do to deal

with the problems caused by the Great Depression?
- ◆ What did the Labour Government of 1945–1951 want to achieve through its programme of reforms?
- ◆ What actions did it take to solve each of the 'Five Giants' identified in the Beveridge Report?
- ◆ What difference did these actions make to the lives of the British people?

Changing Scottish Society 1880–1939	◆ In what ways did the growth of towns and cities change Scottish life in terms of religion, education, leisure and popular culture? ◆ How great a difference did these changes make to people's lives?
The rise of political nationalism	◆ In what ways did Scottish attitudes towards the Union change between 1880 and 1939? ◆ What were the reasons for these changes? ◆ How far did these changes lead to demands for devolution and/or independence?

The growth of nationalism

Growth of national consciousness in Europe	◆ What does the idea of 'nationalism' or 'national identity' mean? ◆ What influences caused national consciousness to grow in Germany or Italy between 1815 and about 1850? ◆ What were the barriers to unification in Germany or Italy? ◆ What political, social and economic factors enabled Germany or Italy to achieve unification as a nation state?
The new nation state in Germany or Italy	◆ What problems faced the new nation state in Germany or Italy? ◆ What was done to overcome these problems, and with what success? ◆ What effects did the growth of nationalist feelings have on the international relations of Germany or Italy between 1871 and 1914?
The rise of fascism in Germany or Italy	◆ What did the idea of 'fascism' mean? ◆ What were the factors that allowed fascists to come to power in Germany or Italy? ◆ What were the features of a fascist state? ◆ In what ways did fascism affect the lives of the German or Italian people?

The large-scale state: the USA

The USA at the end of the First World War	◆ What were the differences in political, social and economic status of the various ethnic groups in the USA after 1918? ◆ What powers did the US constitution give to state and federal governments?
Capitalism and the USA in the 1920s: the growth of federal powers	◆ What is the meaning of the idea of 'laissez-faire'? ◆ What economic policies did Republican governments follow during the 1920s? ◆ In what ways did these policies affect different groups in the USA? ◆ What were the causes of the Wall Street Crash in 1929? ◆ What impact did it have on the US economy and people by 1932? ◆ What changes to federal powers resulted from the Great Depression? ◆ What effects did the New Deal have on the economy during the 1930s?
The Civil Rights movements	◆ Why did American attitudes to immigration change during the 1920s? ◆ What impact did organisations like the Ku Klux Klan have on the lives of minority groups? ◆ Why did the demand for Civil Rights grow after 1945? ◆ What methods did the Civil Rights movements use during the 1950s and 1960s? ◆ In what ways were the activities of black radical protest movements different from those of the civil rights movements? ◆ How great an effect did the activities of all of these groups have on the law, on the powers of the federal governments and on the lives of ethnic minority people?

The large-scale state: Russia

The character of Tsarist government	◆ What does the idea 'autocracy' mean? ◆ What were the features of the Tsarist government system in Russia? ◆ In what ways was life difficult for various social groups in Russia: peasants, town workers and national minorities? ◆ For what reasons was it difficult to oppose or protest against the government?

Challenges to authority	◆ Which groups formed in Russia to oppose the Tsarist state?
	◆ What did the various groups believe and hope to achieve?
	◆ What were the causes of the revolution of 1905?
	◆ Why did the revolution of 1905 fail?
	◆ What changes were there in the Tsarist state after 1905?
	◆ What were the effects of the Dumas and the work of Stolypin on the Tsarist state and the lives of the people?
The revolutions of 1917	◆ In what ways and for what reasons did the Tsarist state begin to collapse by 1917?
	◆ What factors brought about the revolution of February 1917?
	◆ What were the weaknesses of the Provisional Government?
	◆ Why were the Bolsheviks able to seize power in October 1917?
	◆ What factors allowed the Bolsheviks to defeat the White armies and win the Civil War?
	◆ What were the features of the new Soviet State?

Chapter 2

QUALITIES OF A GOOD ESSAY

Everything in this section applies equally to writing an essay under examination conditions and to the Extended Essay. Although you have longer in which to write the Extended Essay and can use your prepared plan, the examiner will be looking for the same qualities in each.

Key Points

Essay structure:

◆ Does your essay have a proper introduction, development and conclusion?

◆ Have you organised your material logically into paragraphs?

◆ Is your approach analytical, or do you simply tell a story?

Knowledge and understanding:

◆ Do you show a good understanding of the historical period?

◆ Does your essay contain enough evidence to answer the question effectively?

◆ Do you **use** the evidence to help answer the question, or do you just show that you have learned some facts?

Analysis of the issue:

◆ How well do you understand what the question asks you to do?

◆ How well do you use your recalled knowledge to judge the strength of an argument or the importance of a factor that caused something to happen?

◆ Do you show that you understand different possible interpretations?

Drawing a conclusion:

◆ At the end, do you answer the question, giving reasons for your answer?

This may all seem very complicated, but it happens quite naturally if you get one thing right at the beginning. The most important step of all is:

Hints and Tips

Read the question

–

What does it ask you to

Do?

This may seem obvious, but many people do not take the trouble to read the question properly. They appear to do little more than glance at it to get a rough idea of the theme – is it about the Scottish Wars of Independence, or the English Civil War, or the growth of democracy, or the unification of Germany or Italy, or the New Deal in the USA or the Bolshevik Revolution of 1917? Having identified the theme, they then write all they know about it, without worrying about whether they are actually answering the question. In some cases, they even seem to have prepared for the examination by memorising essays written as answers to previous questions – perhaps ones they had practised in class – and repeating these regardless of the phrasing of *this year's* question. The examiners refer to this as the 'Blue Peter' approach – 'I don't like the question you have asked, so here is my answer to the one I prepared earlier!'

Those who do this are so eager to show off the facts they have learned that they give up the chance to demonstrate their skills as well. Their answers become narrative or descriptive, often concentrating almost totally on telling the story, with no attempt at historical discussion except, perhaps, briefly at the end. Essays written in this way cannot gain as many marks as those that attempt to answer the question in the paper.

In the Scottish and British History unit of the Later Modern History option, examiners have identified two topics in particular in which candidates sometimes wreck their chances of a good mark by ignoring the question set and writing a prepared answer. These are:

◆ the growth of democracy to 1928, and
◆ the Liberal social reforms of 1906–1914.

For each of these, there are two main themes that the examiners are likely to test, though they will appear with different phrasings.

The Growth of Democracy in Britain to 1928

The two main themes here are:

◆ the extent to which Britain became more democratic during the period stated in the question, which may go up to one of several end dates: 1900, 1911, 1914, 1918, and 1928 have all appeared in previous papers

◆ the reasons that Britain became more democratic during the chosen period.

The trouble is that many candidates come to the examination determined to write an answer on the first theme. They have worked hard to learn the various Acts of Parliament that made Britain more democratic: by extending the franchise, first to more and more men, then to women; by making constituencies more equal in size; by tackling corruption; and by reducing the power of the House of Lords. They may also wish to show their knowledge of increasing public involvement in politics due to the formation of proper political parties and the spread of newspapers. They also remember to note that there were still flaws in the system, even by 1928, which meant Britain could become more democratic still.

All this is fine if the question that is asked is 'To what extent was Britain more democratic in 1928 than it had been in 1850?' But suppose the question is 'Explain **why** Britain became more democratic between 1850 and 1928'. This time, the examiners want you to discuss the **reasons** for the growth in democracy. They expect you to compare the importance of factors like:

◆ Pressure groups, from the Reform League and National Reform Union through the growth of trade unions and the labour movement to the movements for women's suffrage.

◆ The fact that even politicians realised that Britain had changed through the industrial revolution and the growth of towns and cities, so that no-one could claim that in the 1850s Parliament represented even the prosperous classes in Britain, let alone ordinary people.

◆ The spread of political ideas as a result of education and communication, as railways brought people closer together and allowed the growth of national newspapers, but also through national political campaigns and the creation of organised parties.

◆ Arising out of the last two points, the fear that if Parliament did not reform itself it would lead to a revolution, like those that had happened already in Europe, especially in 1848.

◆ Decisions made by politicians in search of political advantage, in the case of some Acts, most obviously the 1867 Reform Act passed by Disraeli to outdo the proposals made by Gladstone, his political rival.

Unfortunately, whenever a question of this kind appears in the examination, some candidates ignore it. They do **not** read the question, but only notice it has something to do with the growth of democracy. This leads them to write something like this:

> 'Britain became more democratic between 1850 and 1928 because Parliament passed a number of Acts …'

and then follows a list of the reforms.

 This is wrong! Do not do it!

Candidates who do this will lose a lot of marks. If you are answering a question of this sort, protect yourself against the temptation to do this by starting off your answer something like this:

'Britain became more democratic between 1850 and 1928 (or whatever date the question mentions) because politicians had to respond to a number of pressures to reform Parliament. These included …'

and you can use the list above as a guide.

The Liberal Social Reforms 1906–1914

Once again, there are only two likely themes:

◆ the reasons that the Liberals decided to pass these reforms;

◆ an assessment of how effective the reforms were in tackling the causes of poverty in Britain (see also *Making a judgement* on page 23).

In the 2005 examination, a question appeared on the first of these themes. The question read, '*How far were the reports on poverty produced by Booth and Rowntree responsible for the Liberal social reforms of 1906-1914?*' Clearly, this was a question about the reasons for the reforms being passed. Good answers discussed the importance of the reports by Booth and Rowntree in influencing the Liberals to pass the reforms, and compared them with other factors, including:

◆ concerns over Britain's 'national efficiency' arising from the rejection of many recruits as unfit during the Boer War;

◆ the influence of social welfare measures in other countries, especially Germany;

◆ changing political opinions within the Liberal Party with the rise of new Liberals such as Lloyd George, who had seen for himself the problems of poverty growing up in Wales;

◆ the political challenge to the Liberals presented by the growth of the Labour movement and the formation of the Labour Party, making some Liberals aware of the need to pass laws to help working people in order to compete for their votes.

Essays that dealt with these points and reached a balanced conclusion scored high marks. Sadly, a fair number of candidates did not approach the question in this way. They had prepared for a question on the effectiveness of the Liberal reforms and either did not read the question properly or chose to ignore it. Their answers often *began* well enough, perhaps something like this:

'The reports of Booth and Rowntree were important in leading to the Liberal reforms because they showed how serious a problem poverty really was and identified some of its causes.'

Some candidates even went on to mention in their introductions some of the other influences outlined above.

But …

they then forgot all about these factors and spent the rest of the essay describing the Liberal reforms and commenting on the extent to which they made life better for the people of Britain.

To repeat what I said about the question on the growth of democracy,

This is wrong! Do not do it!

Those who did this had no chance of receiving pass marks for this question. Keep discussion on the reforms and their results for questions like the example given in *Making a judgement* on page 23. There, this approach is correct because it answers the question in the paper.

Analysing the question

So, how do you work out what the question asks you to do? It may help you to recognise the most common styles of essay question that appear in the examination.

The Direct Question

The simplest style of question is one in which you are asked directly to explain a historical event. Here are some examples from recent examination papers, showing different kinds of possible phrasing:

Example

- *Why did Scotland win the Wars of Independence? (2003)*
- *Explain the decision to abolish the monarchy [in France] in 1792. (2001)*
- *Explain the lack of success of the movements for women's suffrage in achieving their aims by 1914. (2002)*
- *Why did nationalism grow in **either** Germany **or** Italy between 1815 and 1850? (2004)*
- *What was the main threat to Tsarist authority in the late nineteenth century? (2000)*

Although these questions may seem to ask you to describe a process or tell a story, it is impossible to do so without comparing the impact of a number of things that influenced the historical event or process. To take the fourth of the questions above as an example, there was no one factor that caused the growth of nationalism in Germany between 1815 and 1850. Among other factors, it grew because of resentment against French rule during the Napoleonic Wars, which brought some Germans closer together to resist a foreign enemy, because of growing awareness among educated Germans of their cultural heritage and because of the effects of greater economic cooperation between German states. To answer this question properly, it is necessary to consider what part each of these played in the growth of nationalism in Germany and then to reach a conclusion. Although the question does not, at first sight, *appear* to ask you to decide which was the most important factor, a good essay will compare the importance of the various factors and come to a judgement about which had the greatest impact.

For Practice

Task 1

Here are some examples of direct questions. For each one that comes from the period you are studying, identify four factors whose importance you might consider in order to answer the question fully. You will find lists of possible factors with which to compare yours on pages 52–53. These are not the 'right' answers, but simply suggestions of themes which could help to answer these questions.

Medieval History

◆ Why was the Church so important in twelfth-century England and Scotland?

Early Modern History

◆ What was the most important reason for the outbreak of Civil War in England?

Later Modern History

◆ Explain why the franchise in Britain was widened during the period 1850–1928.

◆ What was the most important reason for the rise to power of Hitler in Germany **or** Mussolini in Italy?

◆ Why did the economy of the USA suffer depression in the early 1930s?

◆ Why did the Tsarist state in Russia collapse so quickly in February 1917?

The clue of the isolated factor

This kind of question also asks you to compare the importance of different factors in a historical event or process. But it goes further. It actually tells you what one of the factors is, and asks you to make a judgement about its importance. Here are some examples:

Example

◆ *How important were Louis IX's religious beliefs to his success as king of France? (2001)*

◆ *Assess the importance of financial issues in damaging relations between Crown and Parliament in England between 1603 and 1640. (2003)*

◆ *How important was the Trade Union Movement in the development of the Labour Party up to 1922? (2000)*

◆ *How important was Prussian military strength in the unification of Germany by 1871? (2003)*

◆ *To what extent were the improvements in civil rights for black Americans by 1968 due to the work of the federal government? (2004)*

The usual mistake in this kind of question is to concentrate too much on the factor mentioned in the question. For example, in the question on the causes of the English Civil War, it is not a good idea to write just about the financial problems of the Crown and their effect on relations between the King and Parliament. You should *compare* this factor with others, such as the religious issues at the time. Likewise, in answering the question about the rise of the Labour Party it would be wrong to discuss nothing but the contribution of the Trade Union movement. You should *compare* its importance with that of factors like the socialist organisations, the Co-operative movement and the electoral agreement between the young Labour Party and the Liberals in the 1906 election campaign.

Hints and Tips

It may help you to re-write this kind of question as two parts – a general task and a direct instruction. For example:

1. *How important were Louis IX's religious beliefs to his success as king of France?*

   becomes the task:

   Compare the importance of the reasons why Louis IX was a successful king of France.

   and the instruction:

   Pay special attention to his religious beliefs.

2. *To what extent were the improvements in civil rights for black Americans by 1968 due to the work of the federal government?*

   becomes the task:

   Compare the importance of the reasons for improvements in civil rights for black Americans by 1968.

   and the instruction:

   Pay special attention to the work of the federal government.

So what does 'pay special attention' mean? It means you should do two things in your essay. First, in the main part of the essay you should say a bit more – perhaps an extra 6–10 lines, about the factor named in the question. Second, in your conclusion you should say, with reasons, whether it was or was not the most important factor.

Sometimes, this kind of question is written as a quotation followed by *'Discuss'* or *'How far do you agree?'* or some similar phrase. For example, in 2001 one of the Early Modern History questions read, *'The most serious threat to the Ancien Régime in France was the failure to reform the financial system.'* Do you agree? And in 2000 one of the Later Modern History questions was *'A lack of strong central government in Germany was the main reason for the achievement of power by the Nazi Party in 1933'. Discuss.* It is important to recognise these as nothing more than variations to the format of the Clue of the Isolated Factor. The first one asks you to compare the various factors that threatened the Ancien Régime, paying special attention to failure to reform the financial system and deciding whether it was or was not the most serious threat. For the second, you should compare the importance of the various factors leading to the Nazis taking power in Germany, saying a little more about weak central government and reaching a conclusion about whether it was or was not the main reason.

For Practice

Task 2

Here are some more examples of isolated factor questions. Try your own analysis by breaking each one down into a general task and a specific instruction. It does not matter whether you are studying the period to which the question refers; the process is still the same. Notice the different ways in which the question can be phrased without changing what it asks you to do.

1   To what extent was the baronial revolt against King John the result of his attempts to control them?

2   How far was the French Revolution due to the grievances of the bourgeoisie?

3   Assess the significance of their contribution to the war effort in influencing the British government to grant votes for women in 1918.

4   How important was the personal role of Hitler in Germany **or** Mussolini in Italy in the fascist achievement of power?

5   To what extent was the economic recovery of the later 1930s in the USA due to the New Deal?

6   Evaluate the importance of the Orthodox Church in maintaining Tsarist authority in the period up to 1905.

Now compare your answers with my analyses of these questions on pages 53–54.

Making a judgement

Many questions will ask you to make a judgement about an historical event or about an interpretation of why something happened or what its consequences were. To answer questions of this type, you must weigh up the evidence *for* and *against* a point of view, and come to a *conclusion*.

Example

Questions like this have included:

◆ *To what extent was feudalism in twelfth-century England a partnership for the benefit of the king and the barons? (2001)*

◆ *Do you agree that the Revolution of 1688–1689 had a much greater impact on Scotland than on England? (2002)*

Example *continued* ➤

Example continued

- *How far is it true that Frederick the Great's enlightened policies brought no benefit to his subjects? (2004)*
- *To what extent did the Liberal reforms (1906–1914) improve the lives of the British people? (2003)*
- *Discuss the view that German foreign policy between 1871 and 1914 created more problems than it solved? (2004)*

This kind of question can also be phrased to ask how far you agree with a statement given in a quotation. One such question was, *'A series of weak and half-hearted attempts to deal with the problems of the time.' How far do you agree with this view of the policies of the National Government during the years 1931–1939? (2001).*

Some might take the question above on the Liberal Reforms as an invitation to catalogue the reforms of the Liberal Government: the Children's Charter, Old Age Pensions, Labour Exchanges and the rest, described in detail but without discussion of the issue in the question. To answer the question properly, you must consider – even debate – how much difference these reforms made to the lives of the British people. There is evidence for and against the view that even the most dramatic of these had a large impact on the British people. Take Old Age Pensions, for example. There are those who would argue that they were critical in banishing fear of the workhouse, and who would quote pensioners who blessed Lloyd George for introducing them. Others would point to the low value of the pension and the age restrictions to support an argument that they were less valuable than they appeared at first sight. You should consider evidence on both sides of the argument and come to a balanced judgement about which is the stronger.

For Practice

Task 3

Here are some examples of questions of this type. For each one, identify what you have to do before you can make a judgement. Try it even if it refers to a topic you have not studied – for this task you don't actually need to know about the topic!

1. How far did King David I increase royal authority in Scotland?
2. How successful were Louis XIV's religious policies in France?
3. To what extent did the lives of the Scottish people change between 1880 and 1939 as a result of urbanisation?
4. 'Tsar Nicholas I of Russia was responsible for his own downfall.' Discuss.

You will find my answers for comparison on page 54.

Planning your essay

Once you have worked out what the question is asking you to do, the next step is to organise your information. It can be very tempting, especially if you know a lot about a particular topic, to start at the beginning and try to tell the whole story – and only as a story. Although this approach shows the examiner you have learned plenty of facts, it does not show your understanding of the issue. In other words, it does not help you to answer the question asked.

Suppose you have decided to answer the following question:

*Assess the contribution of **either** Bismarck in Germany **or** Cavour in Italy to national unification.*

Many candidates give in to the temptation to 'say all you know about' Bismarck or Cavour. The effect can be something like this:

Once upon a time there was a man called Bismarck and he became Minister-President in Prussia and he decided to unify Germany and he did it by fighting a series of wars. First there was the war with Denmark . . .

Of course, I exaggerate, but only in the style of writing. This kind of story-telling approach is very common. Followed throughout the essay, it leads to answers whose outlines look something like this:

Bismarck	Cavour
Bismarck becomes Minister-President of Prussia.	Cavour becomes Prime Minister of Piedmont.
Bismarck overcomes liberal opposition to increased taxation to pay for army reforms.	Cavour strengthens Piedmont by bringing in economic and transport reforms.
Bismarck engineers a war with Denmark over Schleswig and Holstein.	Cavour gains the support of Napoleon III at Plombières.
Bismarck isolates and defeats Austria, creating the North German Confederation.	With French support, Cavour provokes Austria into war, resulting in the gain of Lombardy.
Bismarck provokes war with France by doctoring the Ems telegram.	Cavour ignores the departure of Garibaldi for Sicily.
Prussia defeats France and the German Empire is declared.	Cavour accepts Naples and Sicily for Victor Emmanuel and most of Italy is united.
So Bismarck's contribution to German unification was very important.	So Cavour's contribution to Italian unification was very important.

While understandable, these approaches do not lead to good essays which do what the question asks you to do. If you have analysed the question, you will know that it asks you to compare the work of Bismarck or Cavour with the other factors involved and to draw a conclusion from the evidence you present.

To do this effectively, your essay must divide into three sections, each of which has an important part to play. These are the **Introduction**, the **Development** and the **Conclusion**.

The Introduction

There was once an examiner in a Higher English examination who opened an essay paper to find, as the first words in the script, 'By the time you read this I shall be dead.' I don't know what the examiner thought of the rest of the essay, but I am certain that the opening sentence grabbed his or her attention pretty forcefully. It turned out that these words were not a suicide statement by the candidate but the opening words of a letter written to the narrator of a short story, but undoubtedly they had the intended effect – to make the examiner sit up!

Although you are unlikely to have the opportunity for as dramatic an opening line as that, the introduction is your chance to seize the examiner's attention. A good introduction can create a very powerful impression which may last even if the main part of your essay doesn't quite match it. Remember, the examiner will be reading over 200 scripts, many of which include answers on the most popular topics. Large numbers of these will be routine – the examiner may even be feeling a little bored by reading much the same thing, script after script. So, if you can, try to begin with an introduction that does three vital things:

- ◆ It shows you know what the question is about and what it has asked you to do.
- ◆ It does so in a lively and interesting manner and, if appropriate, perhaps even in a dramatic way.
- ◆ It gives you a natural entry into the development stage of the essay.

One approach that does *not* achieve any of these things effectively is to begin your essay with phrases like 'In this essay I am going to …' or 'This essay will look at the reasons for …' or 'By the end of this essay I shall try to reach a conclusion about …' These phrases show a lack of confidence in your material and do not reflect the way that historians write. Whatever words would have followed these phrases will probably stand just as well on their own, and will read more positively.

Example

So, what techniques can you use to achieve the three purposes set out above? Compare these two opening paragraphs in answers to the question on Bismarck's contribution to the unification of Germany.

1 The contribution of Bismarck was very important in helping to bring about the unification of Germany. Other factors like the Zollverein and nationalism were also important. To judge how important Bismarck's contribution was it is necessary to compare it with these other factors.

Example continued ➢

HOW TO PASS HIGHER HISTORY

Example *continued*

2   When Otto von Bismarck was recalled from Paris to become Minister-President of Prussia in 1862, German nationalism was already more than 40 years old. First apparent in the opposition to Napoleon's occupation of the German states, national feeling grew into a movement after 1815. This feeling was encouraged by a growth of interest in German literature and music and by increased economic cooperation between the north German states. By 1848 it was strong enough to make the creation of a united Germany one of the main demands of the revolutionaries.

Which one is more interesting to read? Both introductions show that the writer is aware of the need to mention more than Bismarck to answer the question thoroughly; that is, to place the issue in its broader context. The first one, though, simply says there are other factors to be considered, while the second connects these to each other and to the issue in a way that suggests deeper understanding. The examiner is impressed, and now expects to read a well-informed and well-argued essay.

The same advice applies to those studying Medieval or Early Modern History. Here are a couple of openings to questions from these Options. Which do you think achieves the three aims better?

Example

Medieval

How important were financial reasons for the growth of baronial opposition to King John?

1   There were several reasons for the growth of baronial opposition to King John. These included financial reasons like increased taxes and the way he tried to control the barons by getting them into debt. Other reasons were the loss of Normandy, which meant that some of the barons lost their Norman estates, his efforts to take all power for himself and the way in which he seemed to prefer people from Poitou to English nobles.

2   At Runnymede in Surrey in the year 1215 the barons of England forced the evil King John to sign the Magna Carta to protect the rights of the English people. This traditional view of the barons' rebellion is too simple by far. Though some of the terms of Magna Carta set out rules for the treatment of free people, others reflect the ambitions of the barons themselves. Their rising came from frustration with the ways in which John had tried to control them by getting them into debt, but also from their resentment of his apparent preference of foreign advisers to English nobles and from the fact that many of them had lost their estates when he had lost Normandy to Philip II of France.

Again, both of these are acceptable, but the second is more effective in preparing the way for a strong essay. Notice that some of the points in the two paragraphs are the same, sometimes even in the same words. However, the second version shows connections between the points and also places the baronial revolt in the context of the signing of Magna Carta.

Example

Early Modern History

How far were Charles I's financial policies responsible for his unpopularity in Scotland?

1   Charles I became very unpopular in Scotland during the 1630s partly because his financial policies made several groups of people in Scotland angry. These included Scottish landowners and the people of Edinburgh, who all suffered from these policies. But other causes were also responsible for his unpopularity, including religious differences and the fact that he seemed to ignore Scotland, visiting it only once in fifteen years after he became king.

2   When Charles I became king of Scotland and England, he managed to offend important groups of Scots by his financial policies. To cover the rapidly increasing costs of government, he reclaimed all land given in the name of the king since 1542, so alienating landholders large and small. He also forced the city of Edinburgh to pay the costs of his visit in 1633. As if this were not insult enough, many Scots noted that this was his first visit to his home country in the eight years since he had become king. As an absentee monarch, he had appeared to ignore Scotland completely, not even bothering to consult the Privy Council before taking decisions. While these issues would have been enough to make him unpopular, his approach to religion provoked outright anger in Scotland, as Presbyterians began to fear that he intended to upset the Reformation and bring back the Roman Catholic religion.

The first paragraph is a reasonably strong one, as it identifies several relevant factors. The second is stronger only because it takes some of the points a little further, giving some clues about the argument that is likely to be developed in the main part of the essay.

Summary

In your introduction:

1   **Set out clearly the issue raised in the question to show that you understand what you have to do.**

2   **Identify the main themes you intend to deal with in the rest of the essay.**

3   **Try to create a natural link to the development section.**

4   **Make a special effort to write in an interesting way that will attract the examiner's attention, if you can do so without making it seem artificial.**

For Practice

Practice Section 1

Pick two questions from Tasks 1, 2 and 3, or from the list below, that relate to the period you are studying – one from the Historical Study: Scottish and British, and one from the Historical Study: European and World. For each one:

◆ Analyse the question to explain what it asks you to do.

◆ Write an introductory paragraph that shows clearly you understand the issue in the question and that gives you a natural starting point for the development section of the essay.

Alternative questions

1 To what extent was Henry II of England successful in strengthening the power of the Crown?

2 Assess the effects of the Black Death on European society.

4 Why did the Protestant Reformation succeed in Scotland?

5 How far did Frederick the Great deserve his reputation as an Enlightened Despot?

6 To what extent did Britain become more democratic between 1860 and 1918?

7 How effectively did the Labour Government of 1945–1951 solve the social problems facing Britain after World War II?

8 'Fascism was only able to remain in power through fear.' How far do you agree with this statement with respect to Germany 1933–1939 **or** Italy 1923–1939?

9 To what extent did black Americans achieve equal rights by 1968?

10 Explain the success of the Bolshevik Revolution in Russia in October 1917.

The Development of Your Essay

As its name suggests, this is the section of your essay in which you develop your argument, using the information you have learned (your evidence) to expand on your basic points. It is also the section of the essay where there is the greatest temptation to lapse into narrative or descriptive writing, in your eagerness to show off the range of your knowledge.

Remember

Try to remember that the History course is designed to do more than fill your head with facts about the past. Of course, you are intended to learn historical facts, but not to learn them uselessly, like so many pieces of trivia. You are also expected to learn how to make judgements about events, to weigh up evidence and draw conclusions – to evaluate. The most important factor which will persuade an examiner to give you a high grade is *quality of thought*. The examiner will certainly expect you to present a reasonable quantity of evidence, but will be even more interested in how you use that evidence:

◆ Is the evidence relevant to the issue in the question?

◆ Are the main points presented in a logical order?

◆ Is the evidence used to illustrate or develop points in the argument?

◆ Is there a sign that you are aware of possible alternative interpretations of the evidence?

Organising your evidence

If you have analysed the question accurately and identified the main factors to evaluate, the organisation of your evidence should be quite straightforward.

Suppose you decide to answer the question:

> *How important a contribution did Socialist societies make to the formation of the Labour Party in Britain?*

Your analysis reveals that you need to compare the various factors which led to the formation of the Labour Party, paying special attention to the Socialist societies. You decide to consider three other factors: the growth of the Trade Unions, the extension of the franchise to working-class people and the failure of other parties to address the problems of the working classes. This is made clear in your introduction.

Each of these four factors should now have a section of its own, perhaps a single paragraph or, if necessary, two or three. In this way, information which is related is kept together, giving shape to the essay and providing a natural flow of ideas.

It would still be easy, even after this preparation, to drift into a description of each of the factors in the desire to show your knowledge of the facts. The result would be an account of the beliefs of the Social Democratic Federation and the Fabian Society, followed by an outline of the growth of New Unionism and the dramatic story of the Match Girls' Strike or the 1889 Dock Strike. However, in what way would even an accurate and lively narrative of this sort help to answer the question? It is important to show what part each of these factors played in the creation of the Labour Party. You still display the same knowledge, but by *using* it to illustrate points of analysis like these:

◆ The Socialist societies gave the Labour Party some of its basic beliefs, such as public ownership of industry and transport.

◆ The extension of the franchise created a large number of working-class voters, especially in industrial towns and cities, many of whom came to believe that they needed a party of their own to represent their interests.

◆ In the late nineteenth century, Liberal and Conservative governments seemed to have other priorities, such as Ireland or foreign policy.

◆ The New Unions, whose members included many unskilled and low-paid workers, had the ability to support the new party financially and also provided many of its early leaders.

Each paragraph of your development explains one of these points and illustrates it through your use of points of detail from your knowledge.

If the question is of a different type, asking you to weigh up arguments for and against a viewpoint, the same principle still applies.

Example

Consider this question:

Did the activities of women's rights movements help or hinder the cause of women's suffrage before 1914?

Although you need to know what the activities of women's rights movements were during this period, again it is not sufficient simply to describe them. You must explain the arguments for regarding them as helping and hindering their cause, so that you can reach a balanced conclusion.

You might place points for and against directly against each other, like this:

◆ The non-violent campaigns of the National Union of Women's Suffrage Societies persuaded a number of Members of Parliament to support giving women the vote. Several of them introduced private members' Bills to do so even before 1900. This suggests that such methods helped the cause of women's suffrage.

But

◆ None of these Bills were successful and by the early 1900s it seemed unlikely that these methods alone would convince Parliament to vote for women's suffrage. This suggests that peaceful methods, even if they did not actually hinder the cause, would not work, at least in the short term.

◆ The increasingly violent methods used by the Women's Social and Political Union gained the cause enormous publicity and made the issue a focus for political debate. This suggests that these methods helped towards the achievement of votes for women.

But

◆ These methods led many people (including some women) to argue that the women who carried out acts of violence were irresponsible, and therefore did not deserve the vote. This suggests that they may have hindered progress towards their goal of equal suffrage.

As in the previous essay, use your detailed knowledge to illustrate and expand the points being made. You could give a few examples of the methods used by suffragist and suffragette groups, or of individuals who criticised the violent tactics of Christabel Pankhurst and her followers. The knowledge is valuable, but not for its own sake. It is valuable because it allows you to explain your argument more deeply, using your facts as evidence to strengthen a point.

This process is the same whether you are writing on Medieval, Early Modern or Later Modern History and whether you are writing on Scottish and British or European and World History. If you were answering the question, *How great a contribution did William Wallace make to Scottish victory in the Wars of Independence?* there might be a temptation to tell the whole story in chronological order, starting with the revolt of the barons against Edward I and going through Wallace's rising and its aftermath, the rise of Bruce and his victory at Bannockburn, the Declaration of Arbroath and the final treaty of Northampton. But this would be just a story and would miss the point of the question. An essay of this type would be unlikely to obtain much more than half marks, even though it would contain a lot of useful evidence.

When you realise that the question really asks you to compare the *reasons* for Scottish victory, paying special attention to Wallace, you can use the same evidence much more effectively. Perhaps you identify four main reasons:

◆ Wallace's contribution by leading the Community of the Realm as Guardian of Scotland.

◆ The fact that people from all groups in Scottish society from ordinary people to great lords were involved, making it a truly national campaign.

◆ The leadership of Bruce once he became king, which drew people like Douglas to his side.

◆ The weakness of Edward II making it easier for the Scots to oppose English rule.

Now you can use the information that would otherwise have been used just to tell the story to make an argument about how important each of these was, and to reach a conclusion. Did Wallace make the most important contribution of all, perhaps by keeping the campaign going at a time when Edward I was threatening to subdue all of Scotland? Or was his contribution only temporary, with England back in control of Scotland by the time of Wallace's execution in 1305? In that case, what else was more important?

For Practice

Task 4

Medieval History

In the examination, you have chosen to answer the question below:

> How great an impact did the rule of David I have on Scotland?

Your introduction has outlined how Scotland was governed before David's reign, so placing the question in context, and identified the main issues on which you intend to base your judgement of his impact:

◆ The changes David made to the way in which Scotland was governed, including the introduction of Norman lords.

◆ The economic changes in Scotland during his reign.

◆ The effects of David's policies towards the Church.

◆ Variations in the effects of his rule in different parts of Scotland.

For Practice continued ➢

For Practice *continued*

These are only headings. For each one:

◆ Say whether or not you think it made a significant change to the ways in which Scots lived and were governed, giving a reason for your opinion.

◆ Give two or three examples of detailed information that could be used to illustrate your argument.

You may wish to compare your answers with my ideas on page 55.

Early Modern History

In the examination, you have chosen to answer the question below:

> *To what extent does Frederick the Great of Prussia deserve to be regarded as an Enlightened Despot?*

In your introduction, you have placed the issue in context by explaining differing views of Frederick, mentioning his reputation as an Enlightened Despot but also noting that some historians see his priority more as strengthening the Prussian state. You have identified several themes to include in your essay:

◆ Frederick's policies on religion and their impact on his people.

◆ Frederick's attitudes and policies towards different groups of people, including nobles and serfs.

◆ The motives and results of his policies towards the law, education and social reform.

◆ Frederick's military policies.

These are only headings. For each one:

◆ Say whether or not you think it supports or opposes the view that Frederick was a true Enlightened Despot, giving a reason for your opinion.

◆ Give two or three examples of detailed information that could be used to illustrate your argument.

You may wish to compare your answers with my ideas on pages 56–57.

Later Modern History

In the examination, you have chosen to answer the question below:

> *'The welfare reforms of the Labour Government of 1945–51 were successful in meeting the needs of the British people.' Do you agree?*

In the introduction you have set the issue in context by identifying the 'five giants' of want, ignorance, idleness, disease and squalor, named in the Beveridge Report as the main enemies of the British people. You have claimed that, in order to meet the needs of the people, the government had to defeat these 'five giants'.

For Practice continued ➤

For Practice *continued*

From your learning, you have identified these main points that you want to include in your answer:

◆ the extension of the National Insurance scheme to provide new benefits for people who were elderly, unemployed or ill

◆ the building of new houses to replace those destroyed in the war and to improve the quality of housing in working-class areas

◆ the introduction of the National Health Service in 1948

◆ the encouragement of full employment

◆ the setting up of Grammar Schools and Secondary Modern Schools.

These are only headings. For each one:

◆ Say whether or not you think it was successful in meeting the needs of the people in that area, giving a reason for your opinion.

◆ Give two or three examples of detailed information that could be used to illustrate your argument.

You may wish to compare your answers with my ideas on pages 57–58.

Making links

The structure of your essay will be improved if you can make links between the various factors, arguments and pieces of evidence to show how they relate to each other. This skill is perhaps the most subtle of all the essay writing skills, but its mastery pays rich rewards. There are two ways in which this technique can enhance an essay. Firstly, within a paragraph, it can be used to allow a piece of evidence to reinforce or illustrate a point. Secondly, it can be used to connect paragraphs, to show how their themes are linked, so giving a flow to the argument.

Take the question on the activities of women's rights movements (see page 30). While dealing with the work of the suffragists, you may wish to develop the idea that their methods were showing few signs of success by the early years of the twentieth century. Here are two ways in which similar information can be presented. In the first, the information is given, but is allowed to sit there without working. In effect, it is a narrative.

> The first organisations to campaign for votes for women were known as suffragists. They used peaceful methods like petitions, public meetings and sending letters to Members of Parliament. They claimed that more than half of the MPs had said they supported votes for women. By 1900 some of the MPs had put forward Bills to give women the vote, but these had all failed. Some women began to say that politicians would not do anything if they only used peaceful methods.

In this second version, a little extra detail is added to the evidence, and pieces of information are joined together to make a point.

> Despite over 30 years of campaigning since the formation of the early suffrage societies in the 1860s, the achievement of the vote seemed as distant as ever in 1900. Although the suffragists claimed that over half of the Members of Parliament had told them individually that they favoured votes for women, none of the private Bills of the 1880s and 1890s had succeeded. The more impatient of the women began to argue that the men in power would never give priority to a cause promoted only by letters, speeches and petitions, even if nearly three million people had signed such petitions in only two years (1878–79).

In the second version, there is only a little extra information, but the way in which it is written helps it to be used more effectively. This is done by using simple linking words and phrases. A good example is the second sentence, which joins together the last two sentences of the first version by using the word 'although' to suggest a contrast between two facts – the suffragists' claim that over half of the current Members of Parliament had given them expressions of support and the failure of the various Bills to get through Parliament. This suggests to the examiner that the writer understands the connection more fully than is displayed in the first version. Notice also that the addition of a small amount of extra detail (the number of people who signed suffragist petitions over a two-year period) adds extra weight to the point being made.

In every essay you write there are opportunities to create such links between pieces of evidence. There will also be chances to connect themes by using similar phrases at the beginning of a paragraph. Continuing with the example of women's rights movements, you want to link the two arguments over the value of the suffragette campaign of violence: that it raised the profile of the issue and that it turned some people against the campaign. The discussion of the first point might end like this:

> Actions like the smashing of the shop windows in London's West End, women chaining themselves to the railings outside the Houses of Parliament and Buckingham Palace, or the dramatic suicide of Emily Wilding Davison at the Derby in 1913, kept the cause in the headlines and ensured that the government could never forget the women's demands. They also demonstrated the depth of the women's determination to achieve their aims, reminding many that in 1832 and in 1867 violent actions by men had influenced Parliament to pass reform measures which increased the male franchise.

Instead of going on to say, at the start of the next paragraph, 'some people regarded acts of violence as irresponsible', a more definite link can be created like this:

> Valuable though this publicity was, some argued that the campaign of violence was actually damaging the cause by giving the impression that the militant suffragettes were irresponsible and so did not deserve the vote. Among these was Winston Churchill, who informed a deputation from the Women's Freedom League that their cause was 'marching backwards'.

Notice how the introductory phrase – 'Valuable though this publicity was' – reflects back to the previous paragraph, helping to sustain continuity of thought and to add emphasis to the contrast between the two views of the suffragette actions.

Historical debate

People often ask about the issue raised in the last sentence where it mentions 'the two views …' The examination syllabus, and the marking instructions, refer to candidates 'showing awareness of different interpretations'. Some are concerned this means that for every topic they will have to learn the names of several historians and know what each one has said about it.

Relax! The examiners are more interested in your understanding that there *are* different possible interpretations than in seeing the names of historians in your essay, which can amount to mere name dropping without understanding. The classic example happened when one candidate, anxious to show knowledge of an historian's name wrote, *'World War I began in 1914' (A.J.P. Taylor)*. Hardly a fact that needed to be supported by reference to someone as famous as Professor Taylor! Your understanding of different possible interpretations can be shown just as well by using phrases like 'it can be argued that…' or 'an alternative view might be …' or others that allow you to show contrasts.

Summary

In your development:

1   Organise your ideas in a logical order so that your essay has a proper structure.

2   Give each main idea or theme a paragraph (or more) of its own.

3   Use your detailed knowledge to reinforce or illustrate points, not just to show that you have learned a particular fact.

4   Try to create links between your ideas so that there is a natural flow to your argument.

5   Where you can, show an awareness of historical debate in the sense that you know that evidence can be interpreted in different ways or that evidence can be conflicting.

For Practice

Practice Section 2

1   Take the two questions from Practice Section 1 (see page 28) for which you wrote an introductory paragraph. Write down four main points that you should discuss in your development, together with some examples of detailed information that could be used to develop these points.

2   Write a paragraph about each of these points, showing its importance in discussing the issue raised in the question. As you do so, take care to show the links between each point and the others. Do this by putting connecting sentences at the beginning of each paragraph.

The Conclusion

A strong conclusion to your essay is as important as a strong introduction. It creates a good final impression with the examiner and confirms the quality of your understanding of the issue.

Key Points

A good conclusion does two main jobs:
- It summarises the main points in the argument.
- It gives a direct answer to the question asked.

The last point is very important. Many conclusions restate the main points well enough but come to a stop without providing an answer to the question. To go back to the question on the effectiveness of the Liberal reforms of 1906–14 (see pages 23), such a conclusion could read:

> During the period 1906–14 the Liberals passed reforms to help remove some of the main causes of poverty. The health of children was dealt with through free school meals and medical inspection in schools. The problems of elderly people were tackled through Old Age Pensions and poverty, caused by disease or unemployment, through National Insurance contributions. Some people say that these reforms were the first step towards the Welfare State.

The problem here is that this paragraph does not answer the question, which asked to what extent the reforms improved the lives of the British people. It gives a summary list of some of the major reforms of the period, but does not discuss the issue of their impact on people's lives. Much more impressive would be a conclusion like this, which keeps the question in mind:

> The reforms of the period 1906–14 were certainly targeted more closely on the needs of the people than previous measures had been. It would, however, be an exaggeration to say that they solved all of the problems, for much poverty remained after 1914. Some of the reforms, like free school meals, were not compulsory, while others, such as insurance against unemployment, only affected workers in a few industries. Even the Old Age Pension, welcome though it was, was set at a deliberately low level to encourage people to save for their old age and did not apply to everyone. More effective was the introduction of National Health Insurance to protect workers and their families against loss of income through illness. On balance, the Liberal reforms certainly improved the lives of some of the people, but much poverty remained for later governments to tackle.

This version uses the phrasing of the question as its focus, using the summary of the reforms simply to illustrate the argument. It refers back to the lives of the people and states an opinion about how far these were improved by the reforms. In the last sentence, it gives a direct answer to the question, while avoiding the use of 'I agree . . .' or 'I disagree . . .', 'I think . . .' or 'In my opinion . . .', all of which are unnecessary and may be regarded as immature. It is much better to follow the practice of professional historians and state your opinions confidently as though they were facts.

This remains true where the question asks for a comparison between various factors involved in an issue, as in the question on Bismarck and German Unification considered earlier (pages 24–26). Suppose your assessment is that Bismarck's contribution was the most important factor in the process of unification. A reasonable enough but routine conclusion might read:

> This evidence shows that there were many factors which helped to bring about German unification. These included growing national feeling in Germany, the increasing strength of Prussia and the efficiency of her army, and the errors made by other countries. Bismarck's contribution was the most important because he led Prussia in the victorious wars against Denmark, Austria and France which actually brought the German states together as a united country.

This does mention some of the main factors and does give an answer to the question. However, the factors other than Bismarck's contributions are just listed, without an explanation of what their impact was, while the reason given for choosing Bismarck as being the most important factor is a limited one. All it really says is that he was the leader when unification was achieved, therefore he made the most important contribution. With very little alteration, the same passage could have been used as an introduction.

Here is a more sophisticated approach, reaching the same conclusion but indicating not just which factors were involved but saying why they were important:

> The proclamation of the German Empire in 1871 was the climax of a long process, to which several factors contributed. The growth of nationalism brought about the demand for a united country. Prussian economic development, aided by the Zollverein, allowed the build up of its military power and strengthened its influence, at least among the northern states. Together, these developments made possible a unification under Prussian leadership, but they did not make it certain. What made Bismarck's contribution decisive was his ability to exploit this potential for unity and to overcome the barriers which still lay in the path of unification, especially the opposition of France and Austria. His diplomatic skills in isolating his enemies and his willingness to seize opportunities turned the possibility of unification into reality.

This longer version actually does what the question asks – it assesses Bismarck's contribution in the light of at least some other factors and concludes (though without using the actual word) that his contribution was the most important of all.

Hints and Tips

Of course, it is not necessary to conclude that the factor mentioned in a question is the most important. Remember that in a History essay there is no 'correct' answer. The examiners (who, being historians, are likely to hold differing opinions anyway!) must reward you for showing the skills being tested, whether or not they accept your conclusion. What matters is that your conclusion can be defended and that it arises from a proper evaluation of the evidence.

These ideas can also be shown in examples from Medieval and Early Modern History. If you look again at the first versions of the introductions to the questions on pages 26–27, these, too, could almost have been used as simple conclusions. Here are versions of them that have been adapted slightly for this purpose.

Example

Medieval

How important were financial reasons for the growth of baronial opposition to King John?

There were, therefore, several reasons for the growth of baronial opposition to King John. The financial reasons like increased taxes and the way he tried to control the barons by getting them into debt were important, but so were other reasons like the loss of Normandy, which meant that some of the barons lost their Norman estates, his efforts to take all power for himself and the way in which he seemed to prefer people from Poitou to English nobles.

Early Modern

How far were Charles I's financial policies responsible for his unpopularity in Scotland?

The evidence shows that Charles I's financial policies were very important in making him unpopular in Scotland during the 1630s. His financial policies made several groups of people in Scotland angry, including Scottish landowners and the people of Edinburgh, who all suffered from these policies. But other causes were also responsible for his unpopularity, including religious differences and the fact that he seemed to ignore Scotland, visiting it only once in fifteen years after he became king.

They list the main themes that should be included in a summing up, but their weakness is in making a judgement about the importance of each in answering the question. Here are examples of much stronger conclusions, using exactly the same points, but organised to argue a case.

Example

Medieval

By 1215 the barons could take no more. It was bad enough that John had failed to retain Normandy, costing some barons their estates in northern France. It was worse that to them the king appeared to be determined to strengthen his own position at their expense. They resented the way in which he seemed to prefer people from Poitou to English nobles as his advisers. Although all of these caused discontent, the financial burdens caused by increased taxes and his efforts to control the barons by getting them into debt was the factor than pushed them beyond discontent into rebellion.

Early Modern

Having been born in Scotland should have given Charles I a good chance of being popular in his native land. His failure to achieve such popularity came from a series of misjudgements that showed he had no real understanding of Scotland or its people.

Example continued ➤

Example *continued*

Though his financial policies made several groups of people in Scotland angry, including Scottish landowners and the people of Edinburgh, who all suffered from these policies, the Scots also resented the fact that he seemed to ignore Scotland, visiting it only once in fifteen years after he became king. Charles might have overcome even these mistakes, but his religious policies ended any prospect of this as they made the Scottish people fear that he intended to overturn the Reformation and restore the Roman Catholic Church and the threat of persecution for Protestants. This was what finally provoked open opposition to Charles as shown by the National Covenant.

The conclusion to the Medieval question accepts the factor in the question as the most important, the one on the Early Modern question does not. This does not matter. What does matter is that each conclusion gives a reason for regarding the chosen factor as most important – in the first example the reason given is the financial burdens caused by John's policies and in the second it is the fear of Charles' religious policies overturning the Reformation.

For Practice

Task 5

Take the question about Bismarck (page 24), King John (page 26), or Charles I (page 27). Write a conclusion that mentions the same factors as in my examples above, but argues that:

◆ the economic growth of Prussia, not Bismarck, was the most important factor in German unification or

◆ that the loss of Normandy was the most important reason for baronial opposition to John or

◆ that Charles I's financial policies were the most important reason for his unpopularity in Scotland.

My version of conclusions like these are give on pages 58–59.

Where a question asks you to agree or disagree with a statement, your conclusion should balance the evidence for and against it. For instance, question 4 from Task 3 (page 23) asks if you agree with the statement:

'In the end, Tsar Nicholas II of Russia was responsible for his own downfall.'

Here is one way in which the arguments for and against could be compared.

Many excuses could be made in defence of the Tsar. It could be argued that he was the victim of an outdated system of governing Russia, which he could hardly be expected to reform himself, especially with his upbringing and beliefs. Further, the shocking impact of the First World War on the Russian army and civilians cannot be blamed on the Tsar alone. On the other hand, his willingness to put so much faith in the appalling Rasputin and his failure to respond effectively to the crisis affecting his people turned away many who might have defended him. Nicholas II was not to blame personally for all of Russia's ills, but his errors during the critical months of late 1916 and early 1917 finally lost him the confidence of his people, his throne and eventually his life.

Notice how this conclusion recognises that there could be arguments in favour of different viewpoints before expressing a definite opinion on the question.

Summary

In your conclusion:

1 Summarise the main points in your argument, commenting on how each one relates to the issue in the question.

2 Make a decision about the issue, explaining why you have reached that conclusion. It should be clear that your last sentence is an answer to the question – perhaps even using some of the words in the question to make this clear.

For Practice

Practice Section 3

1 Go back to the two questions you chose for Practice Sections 1 and 2. Write down three main points that you should include in your conclusion, with a brief note of how each relates to the issue raised in the question.

2 Write a concluding paragraph for each essay, explaining these points and giving a clear answer to the question. Try to show that you are aware that it could be possible to argue in favour of a different conclusion.

If you now put together your answers to the three Practice Sections, you should have at least the substantial outlines of three good essays in answer to your chosen questions.

THE EXTENDED ESSAY

Background

The Extended Essay is designed to help you to develop the skills of historical enquiry – planning, researching and reporting – and to take responsibility for some of your own learning. At the same time it lets you study a topic that interests you in more detail than is possible in class time.

The Extended Essay allows you to develop these skills by choosing an issue after discussion with your teacher and carrying out some research to help you build up a plan for your essay. You then have two hours in which to write it up under examination conditions.

Key Points

Purposes

The Extended Essay has several purposes:

◆ To help you to take more responsibility for your own learning.

◆ To help you to develop the skill of planning an essay.

◆ To give you the chance to study in more depth an aspect of the course which interests you.

◆ To let you show off your best work by writing an essay without the strict time limits of Paper 1 and without having to rely on your memory for all the information you need.

The last of these points is especially important. An Extended Essay is no different in style from an essay written in answer to a question in Paper 1. Only the circumstances have changed – *in your favour*.

Choosing an Issue

The rules of the examination place only one restriction on your choice of issue – it must come from the syllabus of the course you are studying. You may choose a title from topics you cover in Paper 1 or from the Special Topic you are taking for Paper 2.

In practice, you would be wise to add a few restrictions of your own. A good issue for an Extended Essay should be one:

◆ which you are confident you understand. The task is challenging enough without picking an area of history you find difficult

◆ in which you have a special interest. This stands to reason. If you are really interested in a topic, you are much more likely to enjoy doing the extra work needed to research it in some depth

◆ on which it is reasonably easy to obtain good evidence, from the History department or from the school or public library, or though sources like the world-wide web

◆ which is phrased as a proper question. This helps you to write an essay using skills like the selection and analysis of evidence, evaluation of historical events, debate and drawing a conclusion.

Give Yourself a Focus

If you choose an issue which is phrased clearly, it can give you a good focus for your work. It helps your research, because you can use it to judge whether the information you find is worth noting. By asking the question, 'Does this help me to reach a conclusion about my issue?' you can avoid going off on side tracks and so save a great deal of valuable time.

A clearly phrased issue will also help when it comes to writing up your essay, because it will help you to select the most relevant evidence and to organise it in a sensible way, so providing a good structure for your argument.

For Practice

Task 6

Medieval History

If you choose to write an Extended Essay on the Crusades, which of these titles might best help you to focus your research and your writing?

1 Who was Richard the Lionheart and what kind of Crusading leader was he?
2 The First Crusade.
3 What were the reasons why Crusaders went to the Holy Land?
4 To what extent was religion the main motive for going on Crusade?
5 Did the Crusaders achieve their aims during the Third Crusade?

Now compare your opinion with my thoughts on page 59.

Early Modern History

If you decided to write an extended essay on Joseph II of the Habsburg Empire, which of these titles might best help you to focus your research and your writing?

1 Who was Joseph II and what did he do for the people of the Habsburg Empire?
2 Jospeh II, Habsburg Emperor.
3 How successful were Joseph II's social reforms in improving the lives of his subjects?
4 Was Joseph II a successful monarch?
5 What changes did Joseph II make to the Habsburg Empire?

Now compare your opinion with my thoughts on pages 59–60.

For Practice continued ➢

THE EXTENDED ESSAY

For Practice *continued*

Later Modern History

If you wanted to write an Extended Essay on the suffragette movement in Britain, which of these titles might best help you to focus your research and your writing?

1   Who was Emmeline Pankhurst and what did she do to help women to gain the vote?
2   The Women's Social and Political Union.
3   How important was the WSPU in helping women to gain the vote?
4   Was the suffragette movement a success?
5   What methods did suffragettes use in this campaign?

Now compare your opinion with my thoughts on page 60.

Common Mistakes

When choosing your issue it is important to make sure you set yourself a fair task, avoiding issues that are too complex or demanding. The temptation to try to impress the examiners by writing on an unusual topic may be attractive. You may be fascinated by the Nazi propaganda campaign aimed at the farmers of Schleswig and Holstein in 1929. But you are unlikely to be able to research such a specialised issue in the time available. Choose a more practicable theme. Don't commit yourself to one which will require more research time than you can really afford, especially as you may well have other examinations to prepare for as well as History.

Besides being over specialised, issues can be too demanding in other ways. Even one which appears to link directly to a major theme in the syllabus can ask too much, not in research, but in planning and writing the essay.

For Practice

Task 7

Suppose you want to write about the rise of the Nazis to power in Germany. Consider these three questions. Which might you cope with and which might present unreasonable demands?

1   Compare the importance of anger over Versailles, the weaknesses of the Weimar Republic, economic depression, political violence and propaganda in explaining the Nazi rise to power.

For Practice continued ➤

For Practice *continued*

2   Discuss the view that the Nazi seizure of power in 1933 was due less to long-term factors than to short-term mistakes made by individuals.

3   Explain why the Nazis came to power in 1933 and why they were able to stay in power until World War II.

Now compare your opinions with mine on page 60. When writing your own issue, it may help to write down several ways in which it could be phrased and choose the one which is most likely to help you to prepare and write your essay to the best of your ability.

Researching your Essay

Once you have identified your issue, your next task is to find enough information to allow you to analyse it and draw a conclusion about it.

It is valuable at this stage to prepare a rough plan by analysing the question, as though you were preparing an essay for the written paper (see above, pages 19–23). This will allow you to identify the various factors or themes involved in your main issue, which will then form the focus for your research. The wide range of topics from which you could choose your Extended Essay issue means that in this section of the book it could be very confusing to offer a range of examples from different areas of the syllabus, making the book very difficult to use. For this reason, I shall use only one example, an issue from the most commonly studied Special Topic, *Appeasement and the Road to War, to 1939*, relating to the appeasement policy followed by Britain during the second half of the 1930s. Examine the issue below:

> *How justified was the British Government in following a policy of appeasement between 1936 and 1939?*

The factors you could consider in tackling this question might include public opinion in Britain during the 1930s, British politicians' attitudes towards Fascism and Communism, the economic depression, the state of the armed forces and the policies of potential allies such as France. These factors now become the main themes about which you are trying to find evidence – though it is as well to remember that you may not have thought of all the possible influences at the start. As you are researching, keep a look out for some other factor that could turn out to be important and affect your conclusions.

Sources

Your starting point in most cases will be your existing knowledge of the topic from your class work, together with any notes and textbooks which your teacher can provide. For the Extended Essay, though, you should be looking to use other sources as well. You may be able to trace suitable books or articles through your school or public library, but often the best place to look for ideas is in the

bibliography in your textbook. This should indicate other books suitable for senior school students, as well as some of the more approachable works written by professional historians.

In choosing your sources it is important not to make unreasonable demands on yourself, by attempting to read too many specialised historical works which could be very long. You do, after all, only have a few weeks in which to carry out your research, and there will be other demands on your time. Nonetheless, it is still good practice to read some history at the highest level you can cope with, because in this way you will be introduced to historical debate.

Historians are always disagreeing – often quite violently. The topic of appeasement, mentioned above, has nearly brought some historians to blows. This makes it important that you understand in what ways they disagree and why they do so. The best way for you to do this is by reading some of the things they have written, to see how different selections or interpretations of evidence can lead people to very different conclusions.

A good rule in judging how much of a serious history book you need to read for this purpose is to remember that a good book shares many of the qualities of a good essay. The author must set out the main issues in the introduction and summarise the argument in the conclusion. In many cases these sections, especially the conclusion, will be the most useful for you to read.

An alternative to reading full-length books is to look for shorter articles. There are several popular historical magazines (at least one is aimed at senior school students) which contain lively articles on topics which may be relevant to your chosen issue. Some articles present a single author's view, while occasionally you may find one which summarises a debate by reviewing the works of several authors. These magazines may also include book reviews, which can be useful examples of debate in action. In recent years a valuable new source is the Internet, on which there are now many sites aimed at school History students. Some of these contain sources that you may not find elsewhere, while others provide factual information or summaries of historical debates. Many candidates now use search engines to find evidence for their Extended Essays.

Taking Notes

There is no single way of taking notes that works for everyone. You must find a style that suits you. At the same time, the system you use must *work*; it must help you to organise your information and allow you to find it when you need it.

Here is a system that works for me. Perhaps it can help you too. When considering the question on appeasement, I would identify these five possible factors:

- British public opinion in the 1930s
- the attitudes of British politicians towards Fascism and Communism
- the economic depression
- the fear of aerial bombing
- the policies of potential allies.

Each of these factors is given a page of its own. While researching, all the information that is found about that factor goes on the same page, with a note to say where it came from, a code to say whether it represents fact (F) or opinion (O) and one to say whether the source is primary (P) or Secondary (S). It could look something like this:

BRITISH PUBLIC OPINION IN THE 1930s

Information	F/O	P/S
Public opinion would not support military action or even economic sanctions against Germany at the time of the re-occupation of the Rhineland. The British people saw Hitler's actions as less aggressive than Mussolini's in Abyssinia. At least he had not invaded another country. *Speech in Parliament by Hugh Dalton, a Labour MP, 20 March 1936*	O	P
February 1933 – Oxford Union debate on the motion that 'This House will in no circumstances fight for King and Country'. The motion was passed. Around this time meetings held by peace movements attracted large crowds. In October 1934 the Peace Pledge Union was founded: within a year 80,000 people had signed a promise not to fight in a war. *David Thomson*, England in the Twentieth Century, *Pelican 1965 pp. 156–157.*	F	S

In this way, all the information related to this factor stays together, which helps in organising it later. The sheets themselves can be rearranged to help put the factors in the most effective order. This makes the original plan for the essay flexible. It can change to reflect your own changing opinions as your research progresses. Having a separate sheet – or more likely several sheets – for each theme also allows for the possibility that a new factor may emerge in the course of the research without confusing the notes. The new one can have a sheet of its own.

Another benefit of organising your material in this way is that it helps you to see at a glance how your work is progressing. It can be very helpful to carry out a quick review from time to time, and to discuss your progress with your teacher, who may notice something that you have missed. In this way, you can obtain good guidance for the next stage.

Example

Looking back to the original five factors for the research on appeasement, part of the way through your research you may have, say, four pages of notes on British public opinion in the 1930s, two each on British politicians' attitudes towards Fascism and Communism and on the state of the armed forces, a few lines on the policies of potential allies and nothing at all on the economic depression or the fear of aerial bombing. This could suggest that you need to concentrate more on areas in which there is a shortage of information – or it could suggest that one or more of these factors is not really important at all, and ought to be dropped from the plan. You would only find out by looking specifically for these areas when you continue your research. Perhaps a new factor, say news of rearmament in Nazi Germany, has appeared in the early stages of your research, so you have given it a separate sheet and are now looking for more information on that as well.

Hints and Tips

Your words or their words?

Often human beings are lazy. We like to do things using the least mental energy possible. While making notes, this shows itself in the temptation to copy out pieces of the source word for word. Try to resist this temptation, as it can lead to writing out large quantities of information without thinking about it. A much better practice is to *summarise* the information in your own words, picking out the points that are important to your issue. This way, you have to think about what the source actually means, so increasing your own understanding of the author's point of view and of the historical issue itself. Even the simple process of making notes, therefore, can contribute to your own learning process.

For Practice

Try this:

1   Copy out this passage, word for word.

> Many British politicians were reluctant to believe that Hitler wanted war in the West; and they regarded war in the East as a potential benefit rather than a threat. They saw Communism as a greater evil than Nazism, and cited Stalin's purges as proof … The Foreign Office, especially Sir Robert Vansittart at its head, warned against Hitler's ambition, but in vain. The government never decided which way it would turn … Britain turned to the League and was disillusioned, looked at France and was looked back at with suspicious eyes, looked to Germany and was treated with flattery, respect and politeness.

Martin Gilbert, Britain and Germany Between the Wars. *(1964).*

2   Write a summary of this passage in your own words, picking out the four points that you think are the most important.

> For Chamberlain, appeasement meant the 'double line' of trying to accommodate Hitler's grievances while building up Britain's defences (especially in the air) so that ultimately the country could negotiate from strength. Chamberlain seemed convinced … that appeasement was the only appropriate policy in dealing with the Fascist dictators in Europe, and the Japanese threat in the Far East. He was dismissive of the role of the League of Nations in international peace-keeping, suspicious of Communist Russia and cynical about the prospects of any US involvement in European affairs.

Peter Neville, Winston Churchill: Statesman or Opportunist? *(1996).*

3   For each of the two passages, sum up the author's argument in no more than two sentences. Which one did you find easier to summarise?

Interpreting the evidence

No matter what issue you choose, you will discover that the evidence does not support only one possible interpretation. This is because History is about the lives of real people, who do not always agree with each other and whose actions arise from complex motives.

If you find that hard to accept, think of the last time you had a difficult decision to make. Suppose several of your friends want you to go to a concert with them, but on the same day your parents plan to visit relatives, some other friends invite you to a party and your neighbours offer to pay you to do some work in their garden. You have also bought a new computer game that you want to try out. Before making your decision you have many things to consider, from your own wishes to a need for money or a wish to avoid offending friends or relatives. When you make up your mind, different people might have different opinions about your reasons – and *your* version of your reasons might be different again! Whether any one of the others involved agrees with your decision may depend on how the decision affects them or on their attitude towards you in the first place.

If that is the case with a decision taken by one person on how to spend one day, explanations of historical events are likely to be even more open to a range of interpretations. Historians' interpretation of the past will depend on their own beliefs and attitudes, on the detailed evidence they have studied and on their selection from that evidence. Their interpretations are also affected by new research which reveals more knowledge on which to base judgements.

Example

Here is one illustration of how historians' interpretations change. Even today, the popular image of life in Britain in the 1930s is that of the depression, summed up in mass unemployment, the Means Test and the Jarrow Marches. At one time, this also represented the accepted historical interpretation of the period, with most historians agreeing that the experience of the '30s was one of total gloom and misery. It is not hard to find evidence of this. Many photographers took pictures of unemployed miners and shipyard workers, newsreels survive which show vividly the misery of those who suffered, and there are many writings from the time, such as George Orwell's *The Road to Wigan Pier*, illustrating this side of British life. This picture is supported further by cold statistical evidence of unemployment in certain parts of Britain.

So strong was this image that when some historians began to suggest it did not show the whole picture people became very angry with them. I was a member of a class at Glasgow University which could not believe it when our lecturer, Dr Derek Aldcroft, told us that for most British people the 1930s were years of rising living standards. We told him this was nonsense, because of the high unemployment rates and the desperate poverty of places like Clydeside and the Newcastle area. His response was to point out that such conditions were confined to those parts of Britain which had depended on the old heavy industries: coal, iron

Example *continued* ➤

Example *continued*

and steel, shipbuilding. Other parts of the country were prosperous, especially the areas of the Midlands and south of England which benefited from the factories which produced the new consumer goods such as cars, radios and washing machines. He showed us evidence that wages in these areas actually rose while prices were falling and that labour-saving goods made life easier and more pleasant. In fact, he argued, more people gained than lost during this period, so his 'optimistic' interpretation was more accurate than the traditional 'pessimistic' interpretation.

You may think, as the class did at the time, that it is unfair to appear to ignore the sufferings of the unemployed. Dr Aldcroft would reply that it is just as unfair to paint a gloomy picture of the whole of Britain because of the bad conditions in some parts of the country. His views, which provoked a great deal of debate, had developed because of new research into areas which previous historians had ignored. That did not necessarily make them right, but because they were based on real evidence they were worthy of respect and consideration.

Each person – you included – must balance the evidence and reach their own conclusion about this or any historical issue. And your conclusion can be as valid as mine or that of any professional historian. What matters is your ability to justify it by considering the evidence and giving sensible reasons for your opinion.

Developing your Plan

As your research progresses, you will learn about the factors involved in your chosen issue in more detail than is possible in your basic course work. This in turn will deepen your understanding of the issue itself and may change your interpretation of it, because you now have more information on which to base an opinion.

This changing knowledge, and perhaps interpretation, will be reflected in changes to your plan. These changes are likely to be at two levels:

◆ You may change the factors you identified originally as being important, by adding new ones, removing ones you no longer consider important or changing the way you have phrased them.

◆ You can now use these factors as headings under which to organise the evidence you have gathered. If you have found out a lot, this may mean you have to make decisions about which evidence is important enough to include and which can be left out. This process of selecting evidence is one which all historians must use, especially when they have a limited space or time in which to write up the results of their research.

It is worth spending a little time on developing the plan in this way, because it helps you to organise your thoughts and will provide a good guide to areas requiring more research. Again, at this stage, your teacher will be able to give you good advice about how to arrange your information most effectively.

By the time you have completed all the research you have time for, you should be able to create a final version of your plan, which will be the basis of the essay you write under examination conditions. This plan must not be more than 200 words long, so you should give some thought to the use you want to make of it.

Common Mistakes

Some people regard the plan as simply a store for all the information they have found out. Their plans contain lists of facts, with no attempt to organise these to support an argument. Such plans do not help them to write well-structured essays which consider the chosen issue, balance the evidence and reach a conclusion. Yours should be written in a way that will help you to do these things.

No format is ideal for everyone, but all plans should follow certain principles:

◆ Your plan must help you to argue a case. To do so convincingly, your ideas must be presented in a logical sequence. Your plan should include the main factors relating to your issue, in the order in which you want to discuss them.

◆ Your plan should free you from the worry of forgetting pieces of evidence that you want to include. Beside or beneath each of your factors, note the information you have chosen to support your point.

◆ Your plan must give an indication of how you are going to introduce your essay and what conclusion you will reach.

You may also decide to use some of your 200 words to remind yourself of any quotations you want to use, such as a particularly well-phrased summary of an historian's argument. If so, be careful that it does not take up more words than you can afford. Even if this is not the case, it is wise to save words by writing in note form, not in sentences.

For Practice

Task 8

Suppose you were preparing to write an essay about my earlier issue:

How justified was the British Government in following a policy of appeasement between 1936 and 1939?

Here are ten pieces of information that might be relevant to this issue. Decide which pieces of evidence should go with each of the five factors listed above, and make a note of each in the smallest number of words that would help you to remember it.

1 The East Fulham by-election of 1933 was won by a Labour Party candidate who was believed to be a pacifist.

2 Several prominent British politicians were very impressed by Hitler. The former Prime Minister, David Lloyd George, who met Hitler in 1936, returned to Britain to describe

For Practice continued ➢

For Practice *continued*

him as a man of supreme quality. The Labour MP and former party leader George Lansbury, who was a pacifist, wrote in 1937 that Hitler would not go to war unless other people pushed him into it.

3   Speaking in London in March 1936, the French Foreign Minister told his audience that the German reoccupation of the Rhineland had to be resisted by force or else growing German power would lead to war.

4   In 1938 several countries in the British Empire, including Canada and South Africa, said that they would not go to war in support of Britain should war break out with Germany over Czechoslovakia.

5   In a debate in the House of Commons in March 1936, Sir Winston Churchill warned that the atmosphere in Europe had changed recently to the extent that war was being regarded as a serious possibility. He also described the German occupation of the Rhineland as a menace to Holland, Belgium and France.

6   In 1935 the League of Nations Union organised a survey which has been nicknamed the 'Peace Ballot'. The historian AJP Taylor challenged the view that it showed the British people as determined to avoid war at any price, pointing out that 6.75 million people out of the 11.5 million who gave their opinions said that war should be used to stop an aggressor.

7   Following the Munich agreement of September 1938, Duff Cooper resigned from his position as First Lord of the Admiralty, saying in the Commons that in his opinion the only way to deal with Hitler was to resist him by force.

8   When Chamberlain arrived at Heston aerodrome from Munich, waving his 'piece of paper' and talking of 'peace in our time', he was greeted by cheering crowds who regarded him as a hero for having prevented war.

9   In 1937 British experts estimated that a German air assault on Britain would last for 60 days, kill 600,000 people and injure another 1,200,000.

10 Many British politicians regarded Communism as a greater threat than Nazi Germany. Their view of brutal Communists was reinforced by the show trials of the 1930s in Stalin's Soviet Union.

My version of what this part of a plan might look like can be found on page 61.

If you organise all of your chosen evidence in this way, your plan will have a structure that will be reflected in the essay itself. You should now be ready to write your essay with confidence, using the writing skills you have been developing for the essay section of the examination.

SOLUTIONS TO TASKS

Task 1

Medieval

Reasons for the importance of the Church in twelfth-century England and Scotland:

◆ Deep religious beliefs of ordinary people, who regarded the Church as their means of getting to heaven.

◆ Social role of the Church as the place people would turn to in time of need (e.g. care for the sick and the poor, education).

◆ Economic role of the Church, especially larger monasteries, which had great estates and were important in the wool trade.

◆ Political role of bishops, archbishops and abbots, who often rose to positions of great power.

Early Modern History

Reasons for the outbreak of Civil War in England:

◆ Charles I's dismissal of Parliament and the period of his personal rule.

◆ Anger at Charles' financial policies, especially issues like Ship Money and wardship.

◆ Dislike and suspicion of Charles' closest advisers, especially Strafford.

◆ Religious grievances and fear that he intended to restore the Roman Catholic Church as the state religion.

Later Modern History

1   Reasons for the extension of the franchise in Britain 1850–1928:

◆ Demands from reformers, e.g. radicals, Labour movement, suffragettes.

◆ Changes in the British economy and society, e.g. industrial and urban growth.

◆ Earlier reforms did not bring disaster – 1832.

◆ Attitudes of politicians, e.g. Disraeli in 1867.

2   Factors allowing the Nazis to take power in Germany:

◆   German resentment of the Versailles Treaty, giving Hitler an obvious issue on which to appear strong.

◆   Weakness in the Weimar Republic – the constitution itself, failure of other parties to work together.

◆   The Nazi image – use of propaganda, violence and local organisation.

◆   The effects of economic crisis – inflation 1923, Depression and unemployment from 1929.

Factors allowing the Fascists to take power in Italy:

◆   Disappointment that Italy did not gain more from the postwar settlement.

◆   Political weakness in the postwar Italian governments leading to street violence and fear of a Communist revolution.

◆   The Fascist image as seen through the Blackshirts.

◆   Mussolini's gamble with the 'March on Rome' and the failure of the government to take decisive action to stop him.

3   Reasons for economic depression in the USA:

◆   Economic policies of Republican governments in the 1920s.

◆   Over reliance on credit to provide prosperity in the 1920s.

◆   Wall Street Crash of October 1929.

◆   Effect of depression in other countries on world trade.

4   Reasons for the collapse of the Tsarist regime in February 1917:

◆   Long term weaknesses within the state – the Tsarist regime had failed to reform itself despite the warning of 1905.

◆   Grievances of peasants, industrial workers and national minorities had not been addressed in the years since 1905.

◆   The impact of the First World War on Russia – casualties, starvation.

◆   Political errors by Nicholas II (e.g. the influence of Rasputin, personal command of the army leading to blame for failure).

Task 2

1   *Task*

◆   Compare the importance of the various reasons for the baronial revolt against King John.

Instruction

◆   Pay special attention to his attempts to control the barons.

2   *Task*

◆   Compare the importance of the factors that caused the outbreak of the French Revolution.

Instruction

◆ Pay special attention to the grievances of the bourgeoisie.

3 *Task*

◆ Compare the importance of the reasons for the granting of votes for women in 1918.

Instruction

◆ Pay special attention to the women's contribution to the war effort.

4 *Task*

◆ Compare the importance of the reasons for the fascist achievement of power in Germany *or* Italy.

Instruction

◆ Pay special attention to the personal role of Hitler *or* Mussolini.

5 *Task*

◆ Compare the importance of the reasons for the recovery of the US economy in the later 1930s.

Instruction

◆ Pay special attention to the contribution of the New Deal.

6 *Task*

◆ Compare the importance of the factors that helped to maintain Tsarist authority in the period up to 1905.

Instruction

◆ Pay special attention to the Orthodox Church.

Task 3

1   Explain what David I did to try to increase royal authority in Scotland.

Identify evidence suggesting he was successful in increasing royal authority.

Identify evidence suggesting he was *not* successful in increasing royal authority.

Compare the strength of the evidence to reach a conclusion.

2   Say what the aims of Louis XIV's religious policies were.

Explain what he did to try to carry out these policies.

Identify arguments and supporting evidence that these policies were successful.

Identify arguments and evidence that they were *not* successful.

Compare the strength of the evidence to reach a conclusion.

3   Explain ways in which urbanisation changed the lives of Scottish people between 1880 and 1939.

Explain ways in which people's lives did *not* change during the period.

Compare the strength of the evidence to reach a conclusion.

4   Identify ways in which Nicholas II can be considered to have been responsible for the Revolution of February 1917.

Explain what other factors helped to cause the Revolution and reach a conclusion about how important his own part was.

Task 4

Medieval History

1   David made the royal government of
Scotland much more effective and
efficient by introducing new types of
official who carried more authority than
previously. His introduction of Norman
nobles, to whom he gave grants of land in
southern Scotland, also strengthened his
power, as these new men were personally
loyal to him.

David's rule improved the economy of
Scotland through the creation of Royal
Burghs with trading privileges. However,
these were concentrated only in certain
parts of the kingdom.

David's rule increased the importance of
the Church, as he became a patron of monasteries and strengthened the power of the
bishops. However, it could be argued that this was a relatively easy task for David as
most Scots were already strongly religious.

Although David's rule did have a great impact on the lives of those living in southern
Scotland, where most of his officials and supporters lived, he had less influence on the
more remote areas of the country, especially the Highlands and islands.

2   Here are a few examples of detailed evidence that could be used to illustrate or develop
these points. Note that they are *only examples*, and many others could have been
chosen.

Royal government
David replaced the old officials known as mormaers with sheriffs who had closer loyalty to
the king. He also introduced new legal officers such as constables and justiciars. When David
gave new Norman nobles large grants of land in Scotland, he also gave them charters to
show that they held the land from the king.

Economic change
During his reign David created fifteen Royal Burghs, making places like Perth and Aberdeen
more able to gain wealth through trade. This practice encouraged trade across the North
Sea with ports on the European continent.

Increasing the influence of the Church
David encouraged the foundation of monasteries, with over twenty being founded during
his reign. These included the Cistercian abbey at Melrose. He also made possible the creation
of three new dioceses in the north of Scotland to increase the influence of the Church.

Variations across Scotland
This is more difficult to support with separate evidence, as the points being made relate to
the previous points (e.g. most of the land given to Norman and English barons was in the
Lowlands, most of the new Royal Burghs were on the east coast).

Early Modern History

1   Frederick offered toleration to people practising any form of Christianity. Though this could be seen as following the ideas of the Enlightenment, it could also be argued that it went against some thinkers who were sceptical about all religions. Frederick's attitude towards Jews was less positive.

Frederick's attitude towards serfdom was certainly Enlightened, as he declared it to be wrong. However, in practice, he failed to follow this through by making it illegal, as he depended sufficiently on his nobles to wish to avoid offending them.

Like many in the period of the Enlightenment, he wanted to make the law fairer and more efficient. In part, though, this was an expression of his Despotism, as a more effective legal system would ensure he remained in control. His social welfare reforms were more positive evidence of an Enlightened approach, as was his interest in agricultural reform.

One element of his rule that emphasises Despotism more than Enlightenment was Frederick's determination to make Prussia a great military power. He invested heavily in the army to improve its efficiency, but it remained organised on traditional lines with most officers being nobles.

2   Here are a few examples of detailed evidence that could be used to illustrate or develop these points. Note that they are *only examples*, and many others could have been chosen.

Religion

Frederick had no strong religious beliefs himself, but offered protection to people of all religious beliefs except Jews, whose willingness to lend money on interest he disapproved of. This led to many refugees coming to Prussia from France and Poland.

Serfdom

Frederick opposed serfdom in theory, and even freed the serfs on his own royal estates in 1763, but his Enlightenment was not strong enough to make him abolish serfdom altogether. Frederick believed in the social order as it stood, and defended the privileges of the nobles. This is more evidence of Despotism than of Enlightenment.

Government and reform

Frederick regarded himself as the 'first servant of the state', whose main motivation was to make Prussia as efficient as possible, largely so that it could be successful in war. This influenced his policies of improving primary education and his interest in agricultural reforms such as crop rotation and new fertilisers under the influence of Dutch and English reformers. This provides some evidence that he was Enlightened.

Military policy

Frederick was a very aggressive military leader who fought several wars. Some of these he began himself, believing it was best to attack in order to avoid being attacked. He more than doubled the size of Prussia during his reign. He was sufficiently Enlightened, or at least practical, to promote talented soldiers who were not noble to become officers during the Seven Years' War, but they were dismissed or given garrison duties when peace returned.

Later Modern History

1   The National Insurance scheme was not completely successful, as some elderly people did not qualify for full pension benefits and the normal rate of unemployment benefit did not meet the needs of some people. However, the 'safety net' of National Assistance meant that almost everyone was entitled to help in time of trouble.

The government's housing policy was not very successful due to the high cost and scarcity of building materials after the war. There was still a serious housing shortage by 1951.

The National Health Service was very successful, despite some problems, because it gave everyone the right to free medical treatment at the point of use.

There were very low levels of unemployment during this period, but this had little to do with government policy and was caused much more by an increase in British exports and by post-war reconstruction which required a large amount of labour.

The education policy, in reality a legacy from the wartime Coalition government, was not successful, because the Secondary Modern Schools were seen as second-class schools, giving those who attended them an inferior education.

2   Here are some examples of detailed information that might be used to develop, illustrate or reinforce these factors. Note that these are by no means the only ones that could have been chosen.

National Insurance

Benefits which were provided included sickness and unemployment benefit, maternity grants, pensions and death grants. Family allowances were paid direct to mothers as many people believed that fathers were likely to squander the money.

Housing

The rate of house building between 1946 and 1951 averaged only 150 000 a year, compared to over 350 000 a year in the period 1934–39.

Many people had to be given temporary accommodation in prefabricated houses.

National Health Service

The service was introduced in the face of strong opposition from the British Medical Association.

The popularity of the service (over five million pairs of spectacles being issued in the first year) meant that it cost much more than expected, forcing the government to introduce charges for spectacles and dental treatment.

Employment

The British share of the world's export trade in manufactured goods went up from 18.6 per cent in 1938 to 25.6 per cent in 1950.

One of the main reasons for this success was that two of Britain's pre-war trading rivals, Germany and Japan, were in no position to compete.

Education

To decide who went to the new types of school, an eleven-plus examination was introduced.

Many middle-class people did not trust the state school system and, if they could afford it, sent their children to independent schools.

Task 5

King John

By 1215 the barons could take no more. They were angry at the way he appeared to be determined to stengthen his own position at their expense. The financial burdens caused by increased taxes and his efforts to control the barons by getting them into debt seemed evidence of this intention. Their feelings were made worse by the way in which he seemed to prefer people from Poitou to English nobles as his advisers. Although all of these caused discontent, the key issue that provoked the barons to rebel was the loss of Normandy, which they saw as bringing disgrace to England as well as costing many of them their estates in France and making them vulnerable to John's policies in England.

Charles I

Having been born in Scotland should have given Charles I a good chance of being popular in his native land. His failure to achieve such popularity came from a series of misjudgements that showed he had no real understanding of Scotland or its people. The Scots resented the fact that he seemed to ignore Scotland, visiting it only once in fifteen years after he became king. They resented his religious policies even more as they made the Scottish people fear that he intended to overturn the Reformation and restore the Roman Catholic Church and the threat of persecution for Protestants. But what really wrecked his chance of popularity in Scotland was his financial policy, which took away the support of the Scottish landowners who lost the lands they had gained since 1542 and angered the people of Edinburgh, who felt penalised by being forced to pay for his one visit to Scotland and for a new parliament hall. These actions lost him the support of those who should have been his greatest friends.

German Unification

Bismarck did indeed make a large contribution to the achievement of German unification. His diplomatic skills allowed the Prussian army to defeat Austria and France without foreign interference, and his eye for an opportunity enabled these wars to take place at the best possible moments for Prussia. Yet he was fortunate enough to be in the position to complete a process which had been going on since national feelings had been aroused by the fight against Napoleon, leading to a demand for unification which had to be satisfied at some point anyway. Even more important were Prussia's economic and industrial growth, which gave it the ability to challenge Austria for leadership in Germany and which supported the existence of the army that made Bismarck's success possible. This, even more than Bismarck's contribution, was the critical factor in bringing about a united Germany.

Task 6

Here are some thoughts on each of the questions and what help they would be to you.

Medieval History

1 Not very helpful. All you have to do is say who Richard was and describe how he led the Crusaders. There is no proper issue to analyse, so you are unlikely to write an essay that is worth a good mark.

2 This is even worse. There is no question here at all, so it would be very difficult to select useful information. What could any conclusion be about?

3 Again, not very helpful. All it asks is for a list of reasons, which would probably lead to a narrative approach. If the question had asked you to *compare* the importance of the reasons, it would have been more helpful.

4 Much more helpful. This asks you to evaluate the importance of religious motives and compare it to the other factors that led people to go on Crusade. This should help you to find relevant evidence and organise it to reach a suitable conclusion.

5 Also a fairly good question, which would have been better with the words 'to what extent…' or 'how far…' at the beginning. You must show an understanding of the Crusaders' aims, balance the arguments for and against judging them to have been successful and then reach a conclusion one way or the other.

Early Modern History

1 Not a question that would help much in planning and researching an essay. All it asks you to do is describe what Joseph did. There is no issue to lead you to a proper conclusion or to help you write a good essay.

2 This is worse still. There is no question to answer, so this would make choosing your evidence difficult and give no clue at all about what to say in a conclusion.

3 Much more helpful. This gives a clear indication that you should compare the evidence that Joseph's social reforms were successful and the evidence that they were less so. It gives good guidance on what your conclusion should be about.

4 Another reasonably good question asking you to consider evidence for and against before reaching a conclusion. It would have been more helpful still with the words 'To what extent …' or 'How far …' at the beginning.

5   A poor question that invites a narrative answer. All it asks for is a list of changes, not a judgement about them. Unlikely to lead to a good essay.

Later Modern History

1   Not very helpful. All you have to do is describe the work of Mrs Pankhurst. There is no real issue to analyse or evaluate, so you are unlikely to write an essay that is worth a good mark.

2   This is even worse. There is no question here at all, so it would be very difficult to know what information would be useful. As for coming to a conclusion, what would it be about?

3   Much more helpful. This question asks you to evaluate the work of the WSPU and compare it to other factors which helped women to gain the vote before coming to a conclusion about the relative importance of the WSPU.

4   Also a good – and challenging – question. Here you must decide what you would regard as success for the suffragette movement, balance the arguments for and against judging it as successful and then reach a conclusion one way or the other.

5   Another bad title, asking only for a description. It does not encourage, or even allow, you to show your skills of evaluation and argument.

Task 7

In fact, none of these is ideal, but a comparison of their demands may surprise you.

1   Although the awkward phrasing makes this question look complicated, actually it is the easiest of the three to research and write. It deals with one issue – why the Nazis were able to come to power – and asks you to compare five important factors. Probably you would want to consider all of these in any essay on the rise of Hitler, so this awkward looking question actually guides your research and helps you plan your essay.

2   A superb question – for a third year university student! You do not have time to research the intricate politics of the months before January 1933. In any case, you might find the issues much too complex given the normal depth of your historical study.

3   Deceptively simple looking – but disastrous. These are really two issues linked by the use of the word 'and':

 ◆   reasons for the Nazi achievement of power

 ◆   reasons why they were able to stay in power.

You cannot do justice to both in one researched essay, even in two hours.

Task 8

One way of connecting the information to your headings (which have been shortened to save a few words) might be as shown below. Notice that it is not possible to write down everything about each of the pieces of information. The words I have used are intended to act as prompts for the memory – even in the Extended Essay you still have to learn some of the facts you want to use as evidence!

- British public opinion:
  - East Fulham by-election
  - 'Peace Ballot': Taylor – 6.75 million for war to stop aggression
  - welcome for Chamberlain after Munich
- Politicians' views on Fascism/Communism:
  - Lloyd George on Hitler
  - Churchill: Rhineland reoccupation a menace to France, Belgium, Holland
  - Communism more dangerous than Nazism
  - Duff Cooper's resignation
- Economic depression
- Fear of bombing:
  - experts: 60 days; 600,000 dead; 1.2 million injured
- Policies of allies:
  - 1936 France for force over Rhineland
  - 1938 Empire countries would not support war

Notice that there are more points for some headings than for others. The economic depression has none at all. More research indicated there!

SECTION 2

Source Handling Skills

SOURCE HANDLING SKILLS

The Special Topic which you study forms the source-based part of the examination, intended to test your ability to work with historical sources of various kinds and to relate these to your recalled knowledge.

What do you need to know?

In order to use your source handling skills effectively, you need a good knowledge of the facts about your Special Topic. As with the section on essay writing, this book cannot give you every piece of information you need to know, but below is a summary of the issues you need to know about, divided by Special Topic. As before, this is not a complete list, but should be a reasonable guide.

Historical Special Topic	What you need to know
Norman Conquest and Expansion (1050–1153)	◆ Why did the Normans become involved in overseas expansion? ◆ What were the features of Norman rule in southern Italy? ◆ What claims did William of Normandy and Harold Godwinson have to the throne of England? ◆ Why was William's invasion of England successful? ◆ What impact did Norman rule have on life in England, especially on government, landholding, the ordinary people and the Church? ◆ How far did David I introduce a Norman way of life into Scotland? ◆ What were the features of the Anglo-Norman rule of Henry I in England? How effectively did Henry rule England? ◆ To what extent was there a 'Norman achievement'?
The Crusades (1096–1204)	◆ What were the causes of the First Crusade? What were the motives of those who went on Crusade, both rich and poor? ◆ What was meant by 'the crusading ideal'? How far did it change over the period? ◆ What were the reasons for the failure of the People's Crusade? What obstacles did the Princes' Crusade face? Why were they successful in taking Jerusalem and setting up the Latin Kingdom? What were the effects of this on the trade of the Mediterranean?

Historical Special Topic	What you need to know
	◆ What provoked the Third Crusade? What issues divided the Crusaders? How important were personalities in the outcome of the Crusade, especially Richard I and Saladin?
	◆ What were the effects of the Crusades on life in Palestine and in Europe?
Scotland: 1689–1715	◆ What effects did the Revolution Settlement of 1688–1689 have on Scotland, especially on government and the Church?
	◆ What were the causes of tension between England and Scotland between 1689 and 1707? What were the options for ending this tension?
	◆ What were the main arguments in the debate for and against an 'incorporating' or a 'federal' union? What were the reasons for the passing of the Act of Union?
	◆ In what ways did the Act of Union affect Scotland in the years after its passage? How successful was the Union in addressing political, economic and religious issues in Scotland?
	◆ Why did a Jacobite rebellion take place in 1715?
The Atlantic Slave Trade	◆ What effects did the slave trade have on tribal societies in Africa? What resistance was there to the slave trade? What were the features of the slave societies in the New World?
	◆ What attitudes were expressed towards the slave trade in eighteenth-century Britain? What reasons were there for such attitudes?
	◆ Why did views towards the slave trade change in Britain? What methods did the abolitionists use to promote their cause? What defences did pro-slavery groups put forward?
	◆ What were the main reaons for the abolition of the slave trade in 1807? What were the effects of abolition on Britain and on British trade?
The American Revolution	◆ What were the main features of British rule in the American colonies? Why did challenges to British control come about between 1763 and 1775?
	◆ Why did it prove impossible to resolve the problems between Britain and its colonies peacefully? What were the results of the Declaration of Independence within the colonies?
	◆ What problems did Britain face in fighting the Revolutionary War? How important was foreign intervention in the eventual British defeat?
	◆ What impact did the outcome of the war have on Canada?
	◆ What were the main principles of the Constitution of 1787?

Historical Special Topic	What you need to know
Patterns of Migration: Scotland (1830s–1930s)	◆ Why did migration take place into Scotland, from Scotland and within Scotland during the period? ◆ What were the effects on Scottish life of the Irish immigration, especially during the 1830s and 1840s? ◆ What impact did this immigration have on town and city life, law and order, housing, religion and education? ◆ How well did Irish migrants become part of the Scottish community by the 1930s? How closely did their experiences match those of European immigrant groups during the same period? ◆ What experiences did Scots emigrants have during the period? In particular, how successful were they and to what extent did they keep a Scottish identity? ◆ How seriously did emigration affect Scotland?

Appeasement and the Road to War	◆ In what ways did the foreign policies of Hitler and Mussolini affect international relations in Europe? What issues did the other powers like Britain and France now have to face?
	◆ What were the effects of Mussolini's invasion of Abyssinia, and the failure of the League of Nations sanctions, on Britain and France?
	◆ For what reasons did Britain adopt the policy of 'appeasement'? What was the policy of appeasement, and in what ways was it intended to improve international relations?
	◆ To what extent did public and political support for appeasement change between 1936 and 1939?
	◆ In what ways did these crises affect relations between the Great Powers:
	  ◆ Hitler's re-occupation of the Rhineland in March 1936;
	  ◆ The Spanish Civil War
	  ◆ The Anschluss of March 1938
	  ◆ The Czech crisis of May–September 1938?
	◆ How successful was the appeasement policy in responding to these crises?
	◆ Why did the British government abandon appeasement during 1939? Why did the Second World War break out in September 1939?

The Origins and Development of the Cold War, 1945–1985	◆ For what reasons did tension develop between East and West during the period 1945–1955?
	◆ In what ways did the following crises illustrate tensions between the Superpowers between 1956 and 1970:
	  ◆ The Hungarian uprising of 1956
	  ◆ The Berlin Crisis of 1960
	  ◆ The Cuban Missile Crisis of 1962
	  ◆ The Vietnam War
	  ◆ The crisis in Czechoslovakia in 1968?

Historical Special Topic	What you need to know
	◆ Why did none of these crises lead to a nuclear war between the Warsaw Pact and NATO? In what ways did superpower leadership change by the 1970s? ◆ What threats were there to international peace between 1975 and 1985? In what ways did the superpowers co-operate to resolve these without a major war?
Ireland 1900–1985: A Divided Identity	◆ Why did demands for Home Rule grow in Ireland between 1900 and 1912? In what ways were the northern counties different from the rest of Ireland? ◆ In what ways did the nationalist and unionist communities respond to the Home Rule Bill? What arguments took place over Irish involvement in the First World War? ◆ In what ways did nationalism develop in Ireland up to 1916? Why was the Easter Rising unsuccessful? What effects did the Rising and its aftermath have on Ireland? ◆ Why was Sinn Féin successful in the 1918 election? Why did demands for independence lead to the Anglo-Irish War? ◆ In what ways did the Government of Ireland Act and the Treaty of 1921 attempt to solve the problem of governing Ireland? How successful were they? ◆ Why did the Irish Civil War of 1922–1923 take place? ◆ What have been the long-term results for Ireland, and especially Ulster, of the creation of the Irish Free State and later the Republic? Why did the Civil Rights campaign begin in Ulster in 1968 and why did it lead to a long period of violence?

Chapter 6

WHAT YOU ARE GIVEN

No matter what Historical Special Topic you are studying, this section of the examination contains *five* source extracts, which may include *primary* and *secondary* sources. You are also told where each source came from: its provenance. This may include the name of the author, a description of the type of source, the title of the source (if it has one) and the date of its creation or publication. This is intended to help you to decide if it is a primary or secondary source and if the author was involved personally in the events or issue to which the source refers.

Primary Sources and Secondary Sources

A primary source is either one which was written or created at the time of the events concerned, or one which was written later by someone who was alive at the time, reflecting on their own memories of the period. Among the contemporary sources there may be speeches, letters, newspaper articles, cartoons, posters, pictures or books. Later works which can still be regarded as primary because they represent first-hand knowledge are likely to be books, often memoirs, published in later years. When you see that a book was published 20, 30 or more years after the events which it discusses, do not assume that this makes it a secondary source. If it describes and comments on personal experiences, it should be regarded as a primary source.

Secondary sources are ones which are not based on personal involvement at the time, but which interpret historical events from a study of the surviving evidence. Typically, these are taken from articles or books written by historians who have studied the period concerned.

Differences Between Primary and Secondary Sources

The historian Eric Hobsbawm once wrote, 'What the contemporary observer sees is not necessarily the truth, but the historian ignores it at his peril.' *Industry and Empire* (1968). This explains why you are asked to evaluate contemporary sources. Just as historians interpret historical evidence in different ways, so people who participate in the events have different ways of seeing the events in which they were involved.

Example

If you doubt this, think of a simple event like a traffic accident. Apart from the drivers, whose opinions are likely to be coloured by personal involvement, there may be half a dozen witnesses whose views of the accident will vary depending on how far they were from the collision, which way they were facing, how good their eyesight is, how much attention they were paying and a host of other factors. The police officer investigating has to take statements from them all, doubtless containing some conflicting evidence, and reach a balanced conclusion on what actually happened and who, if anyone, was to blame.

Witnesses to historic events are subject to even more influences than those of witnesses to an accident. Even those who are involved almost certainly do not know the whole story. In any case, their accounts are likely to be biased by their own prejudices and by the natural desire to appear in a good light themselves. Those whose involvement is less direct have to base their opinions on what they learn from public statements or through the media. To take an example from 2005, interpretations of events in Iraq will be very different when given by people whose knowledge of these events comes in different ways. A future historian may be faced with many versions of these events from, for example:

◆ President George W. Bush of the United States of America

◆ the Iraqi former President, Saddam Hussein

◆ a Shia Muslim cleric from Basra in southern Iraq

◆ individual Iraqi people from different parts of the country, who have lost homes and family members during the fighting

◆ a member of the Iraqi police force in Baghdad

◆ a member of the British army who has been attacked during a violent protest against foreign intervention

◆ a French journalist who has visited cities in the Kurdish area of northern Iraq

◆ people in Britain who have read about the events in the newspapers and watched television reports of them.

It would hardly be realistic to expect all of these people to agree. The task of the historian is to evaluate their evidence and to try to come as close to the truth as possible. The same is true of any period in history.

Hints and Tips

It is not correct, then, to form the equation: primary = accurate and reliable. The primary source may tell you as much about the author as it does about the issue to which it relates. Avoid the temptation to assume that a primary source is right and a secondary source about the same topic is wrong, just because the primary source was written nearer the time.

Of course, the fact that a secondary source is written by someone who has studied the period gives it both advantages and disadvantages. One advantage is the fact that the historian does not have the immediate, often emotional, involvement in the events and the passage of time provides the ultimate result of events, giving the historian the benefit of hindsight. The secondary source is also based on a study of a wider range of evidence, allowing the writer to compare the primary accounts and test one piece of evidence against others, which should allow a more accurate interpretation to be made. As with primary sources, this does not lead to the conclusion that secondary = accurate, because the historian may also be biased or may not have access to all the important evidence. The secondary source is a considered to be an interpretation, but as you know (see pages 48–49) interpretations tend to change as fresh evidence is uncovered.

The best advice on evaluating sources (primary and secondary) is to read them in the light of your own understanding of the period being studied. After all, your interpretation is just as valid as mine or anyone else's, as long as you can justify it by careful assessment of the evidence.

Key Points

Types of Question

Questions in this part of the examination are designed to test how well you can:

◆ evaluate a range of primary and secondary sources, taking into account their origin and purpose

◆ interpret the content of the sources

◆ compare sources

◆ relate sources accurately to historical developments and events through recall

◆ present a balanced view of a source or sources

◆ show understanding of the wider context when evaluating or comparing sources.

(Adapted from the performance criteria for the examination as published by the Scottish Qualifications Authority.)

In each Historical Special Topic, these skills will be tested through *five* questions, each one worth between 4 and 8 marks. The pattern will be the same in every Special Topic, to make certain that everyone has, as nearly as possible, a paper of the same level of difficulty. The questions are of three types:

◆ Questions which ask you to *evaluate* a source.

◆ Questions which ask you to *compare* two sources.

◆ Questions which ask you to *place a source or sources in their historical context*.

EVALUATING SOURCES

You will have to answer *one* question of this kind in the examination, and it will be worth either 4 or 5 marks. It will probably be phrased in one of the following ways:

◆   *How useful/valuable is Source X as evidence of … ?*

◆   *How useful/valuable is Source X in understanding … ?*

◆   *Assess the value of Source X in explaining …*

◆   *Evaluate Source X as evidence of …*

◆   *How reliable is Source X in explaining … ?*

Questions of this kind are easy to spot in the examination. Beneath the question you will find these instructions:

In reaching a conclusion you should refer to:

◆   *the origin and possible purpose of the source*

◆   *the content of the source*

◆   *recalled knowledge.*

It is usually easy to identify the origin of a source, as you are given information about this above the extract. However, it may not always be easy to identify a purpose beyond the wish to communicate the author's opinion or to sell a newspaper. It is more important to be able to identify any possible bias, on which you may be able to comment depending on what you know about the author. A member of the International Brigade in Spain, for example, is likely to be anti-fascist and anti-appeasement, while a member of the British government is likely to want to defend government policy.

To help you see how to answer a question like this well, it is perhaps best to take a real example. This Source and question are taken from the 2004 examination, from the *Ireland 1900–1985* Special Topic.

Example

Source A: from Police Intelligence reports from County Cavan, 1914.

> All classes displayed a strong patriotic and anti-German feeling, and joined irrespective of creed and politics in giving a hearty send-off to reservists and recruits when leaving to join the army. Nevertheless considerable unrest prevailed in both the unionist and nationalist ranks as to the action the government would take with regard to the Home Rule Bill …
>
> The present war is popular with all classes save a few Sinn Féiners, and there is not the slightest sympathy with the Germans; all sections are working cordially together to raise funds for the assistance of dependants of soldiers and sailors involved in the war.

How useful is **Source A** as evidence of Irish attitudes towards participation in the First World War? (5 marks)

In reaching a conclusion you should refer to:

◆   *the origin and possible purpose of the source*

◆   *the content of the source*

◆   *recalled knowledge.*

A good answer to this question would say that this is likely to be of considerable value as it is a primary source (written at the time) and is from an official source, whose purpose was to help the government to assess the level of support in Ireland for the war. You might also know that County Cavan is towards the north of Ireland but most of its people were Roman Catholic, so might have had nationalist sympathies.

In referring to the content of the source, you could write something like this:

> Source A reported that, with the exception of some extreme nationalists ('a few Sinn Féiners') Irish support for the war effort was strong. This is shown by the references to anti-German feelings as shown in the send-offs given to soldiers leaving for the war and in the way people were working together to raise money for soldiers' families.

Note how this part of the answer does two things. First, it says what the *overall* view is in the source (that there was general support for the war effort) and then gives a couple of points of detail to say what made the writer *decide* that was what the source was saying.

Now it is time to carry out the evaluation of the usefulness of the source by testing this view against recalled knowledge. Points that could be made here might include the strong support for the war effort from Sir Edward Carson and the Unionists as well as John Redmond, leader of the Home Rule supporters, who campaigned for recruits to join the forces. There was some opposition from extreme nationalists such as Patrick Pearse, but he and his followers were in a minority. As this evidence agrees with the main themes in the source, it would be a reasonable conclusion that the source does provide useful evidence of Irish attitudes towards participation in the war, at least in 1914. Wherever possible, try to avoid separating the points from the source and the points from recall, but use the recall to comment on points from the source. In this example, it would be useful to bring in some recall to comment on the source's claim that support for the war effort was strong. The paragraph above would then become even stronger, like this:

> When Source A reported that, with the exception of some extreme nationalists ('a few Sinn Féiners') Irish support for the war effort was strong, its judgement was accurate, as was demonstrated by the campaign of the nationalist leader, John Redmond, to encourage Irishmen to volunteer. This supports the references in the source to anti-German feelings as shown in the send-offs given to soldiers leaving for the war and in the way people were working together to raise money for soldiers' families.

This allows you to show your understanding by integrating evidence from the source and from recall and using this to make a point of evaluation – 'its judgement was accurate'.

! **Here is another example, taken from the Special Topic *Appeasement and the Road to War* in the 2002 examination.**

Example

Source A: from *Old Men Forget*, the autobiography of Duff Cooper (1953).

> But the occupation of the Rhineland went even further than the already familiar denunciations of the Treaty of Versailles. It was a flagrant, unprovoked violation of the Treaty of Locarno, which had been freely negotiated and agreed upon with the full and openly expressed approval of the German people. The average Englishman was quite unable to appreciate the significance of Hitler's military occupation of the Rhineland. 'Why shouldn't the Germans move soldiers about in their own country?' was the not unnatural reaction of the ignorant. They could not understand that by this act a ruthless dictator had torn into shreds a treaty upon which the peace of Europe depended. Nor was this lack of understanding confined to the less educated class.

How useful is **Source A** as evidence of British opinion towards the German reoccupation of the Rhineland in March 1936? (5 marks)

Though in 2002 the extra instructions, or prompts, were not yet included in the paper, examiners expected the same kind of answer.

Here is a sample of what a good answer might have said.

> Though not published until 1953, Source A is a primary source, giving the opinions of Duff Cooper, who was Secretary of State for War in 1936. As an autobiography, it was written to justify his own part in the events of the time, so may not reflect exactly what he thought at the time, but rather what he thought would look best later. Cooper did become an opponent of appeasement, and resigned from the government in protest at the policy, but not until 1938.

> In this extract, he is very critical of Hitler's reoccupation of the Rhineland because it was an act of aggression, not only against the hated Treaty of Versailles, but also against the Locarno Treaty, which Germany had signed willingly. Cooper also says that most people in England, including educated people, were wrong in seeing the reoccupation of the

Rhineland as not very serious. He was right that the majority of people did take this view, most people seeing Hitler's action as something that had to happen sooner or later. Most British people would not have supported military action against Germany, as they felt Hitler was only correcting a harsh treaty. Only a few people, including some members of the Labour Party, spoke out against Hitler at this time.

Source A is useful evidence for two reasons. It represents a minority view, even if written with hindsight, and it explains critically the majority view that Hitler had done nothing wrong.

This answer does everything that the question asks:

◆ It comments on the authorship, origin and purpose of the source (using some recall about the author to make a point).

◆ It summarises the argument in the source, giving some details to support the interpretation (that the author was against the reoccupation of the Rhineland and that he was critical of other people's attitudes).

◆ It provides some recalled knowledge against which to judge the accuracy of the source's argument.

◆ It gives a short conclusion that answers the question.

To show that the method is the same even if the question looks a little different, here is a question that might come up in the Special Topic, *The Origins and Development of the Cold War*.

> ### Example
>
> **Source A:**   from a speech by President John F. Kennedy in West Berlin, 26 June 1963.
>
> > Today, in the world of freedom, the proudest boast is Ich bin ein Berliner [I am a Berliner].
> >
> > There are many people in the world who do not understand what is the great issue between the free world and Communists. Let them come to Berlin. And there are some who say in Europe and elsewhere that we can work with the Communists. Let them come to Berlin. Freedom has many difficulties and democracy is not perfect; but we never had to put up a wall to keep our people in. I know of no city which has been besieged for 18 years and still lives with the vitality, force, hope and determination of this city of West Berlin . . .
> >
> > In 18 years of peace and good faith this generation of Germans has earned the right to be free, including the right to unite their family and nation in lasting peace with the goodwill of all people.
>
> Assess the value of **Source A** as evidence of the policy of the United States towards Berlin in 1963. (5 marks)
>
> *In reaching a conclusion you should refer to:*
> - *the origin and possible purpose of the source*
> - *the content of the source*
> - *recalled knowledge.*

In referring to origin and possible purpose, you could say:

> This was one of the most famous speeches ever made by President Kennedy, whose purpose was to encourage the people of West Berlin and West Germany at a time when there was great fear of a potential Warsaw Pact attack on West Germany and to warn the Soviet Union not to be tempted into any aggressive act.

There is plenty to say about the content of the speech and what it tells you about American foreign policy. For example:

> In this source, President Kennedy made it clear that he believed there were real differences between the Western powers and the Soviet *bloc* and that the Western way of life was superior to that of the Communist countries. He pointed to the building of the Berlin Wall as evidence of that superiority, as such action had never been needed to prevent people leaving the West. He also praised the people of West Berlin for standing up to the pressures from the East, and stated his opinion that Germany ought to be allowed to reunite.

The sentence about the origin and purpose actually contains some recall, but you could also refer to the crisis the building of the wall had caused between the Superpowers and to the fact that the speech made the Soviets very aware that American attention was on West Berlin and that this may have prevented them from any attempt at a surprise attack.

Summary

In dealing with source evaluation questions:

1 Show that you understand what the question asks you to do.

2 Comment on the origin and, if relevant, the purpose of the source.

3 Show that you understand the main point the author is trying to communicate, and support this with points of detail.

4 Use points from recalled knowledge to comment on how her or his view compares with your knowledge of the issue

5 Write a short conclusion that answers the question.

For Practice

Task 1

Here are questions asking you to evaluate three sources, one from Medieval History Special Topic, *The Crusades*, one from Early Modern History Special Topic, *The American Revolution*, and one from Later Modern History Special Topic, *Appeasement and the Road to War*.

For the topic you are studying:

◆ say what the overall view of the source is on the issue in the question

◆ list three points of detail from the source that made you *decide* that was the overall view

◆ give two points of information from recalled knowledge that would help you make a judgement about the usefulness or value of the source in terms of the issue in the question.

You can compare your ideas with mine on pages 101–102.

The Crusades 1096–1204

Source A: from a letter from Pope Urban II to the people of Flanders, April 1096.

> The barbarians in their frenzy have invaded and ravaged the churches of God in the eastern region. Worse still, they have seized the Holy City of Christ [Jerusalem], made great by his passion and resurrection, and – it is blasphemy to say it – they have sold her and her churches into hateful slavery.

How valuable is **Source A** as evidence of the reasons for the calling of the First Crusade?

(5 marks)

For Practice continued ➤

For Practice continued

The American Revolution

Source B: from a speech by Lord Lyttelton in Parliament, 10 February 1766.

It is said that they [the American colonies] will not accept the Stamp Act as it is an internal tax. If this is true, the same reasoning applies to all Acts of Parliament … The only question is whether the American colonies are part of the dominions of Great Britain. If not, the parliament has no power over them. It they are, they must be objects of our law making. By making them exempt from one law, you declare them no longer subjects of Great Britain, and make them small independent communities not entitled to your protection.

Assess the value of **Source B** as evidence of British attitudes towards the American colonies in the 1760s. (5 marks)

Appeasement and the Road to War, to 1939

Source C: from a letter from Thomas Moore, a Conservative MP, to *The Times*, 17 March 1938.

If the Austrian people had not welcomed this union, physical opposition and bloodshed must have occurred. That so far there has been none proves the inherent desire of the two nations to secure the *Anschluss* of which they have been so long deprived by the determined interference of the leading European powers . . . [Austria] has free markets for her raw materials and manufactured goods, but, more important still, she is removed as a source of friction and discord from international relationships.

How useful is **Source C** as evidence of British public opinion towards the Anschluss of March 1938? (5 marks)

Sometimes the source you are given may be a visual source. Examples of these in recent examinations have included maps, photographs, posters and political cartoons. Although some people worry about the difficulty of picking out evidence from such a source, especially a cartoon which is intended to be humorous, you should use it in just the same way as you would a written source. For cartoons, the fact that it is meant to be funny often makes it easier to use, as the cartoonist has to make the point very clearly for people to laugh at it. Here is one of the most famous of all cartoons, full of points you can pick out.

Example

Source X: a cartoon by Ernest H. Shepard in *Punch*, March 1936.

THE GOOSE-STEP.

"GOOSEY GOOSEY GANDER,
WHITHER DOST THOU WANDER?"
"ONLY THROUGH THE RHINELAND—
PRAY EXCUSE MY BLUNDER!"

The question could be exactly the same as the one on the Duff Cooper speech earlier (see page 74):

How useful is **Source X** as evidence of British opinion towards the German reoccupation of the Rhineland in March 1936? (5 marks)

In reaching a conclusion you should refer to:

◆ *the origin and possible purpose of the source*

◆ *the content of the source*

◆ *recalled knowledge.*

Again, this is a primary source, drawn at the time and published in a popular magazine.

So what attitude did Ernest Shepard take towards the Rhineland in drawing his cartoon? Look at the detail:

◆ Germany is shown as a heavily armed goose, though it has a laurel branch, the sign of peace, in its mouth along with the label *Pax Germanica* which means 'German peace'.

◆ The windows of the houses are filled with swastika flags, suggesting that the people of the area welcomed the German reoccupation.

◆ The goose is shown trampling on the torn up Treaty of Locarno.

◆ The goose itself is a visual joke because the German army used the goose step as its marching step.

◆ The use of the word 'Only' in the caption suggests the action is not a very serious one.

All of this suggests that Shepard was against the reoccupation and was trying to persuade people of how dangerous a move Hitler had made. If you made *that* point, and used even two or three of the pieces of evidence above to explain your reasons for saying so, you would be well on the way to gaining a good mark. To go the rest of the way, you need to use your recalled knowledge to make the judgement asked for in the question – how useful is this as evidence of British opinion? You can use exactly the same kinds of recalled information as in the answer to the question about Duff Cooper's speech – Shepard, in showing Germany as militaristic and aggressive, did not reflect the common view that her action was justified, but was much closer to the minority view of Churchill and his colleagues who wanted to oppose Hitler as early as possible. Other supporting points of recall could include:

◆ This action did destroy the agreement made at Locarno in 1926 as well as breaking the terms of the Treaty of Versailles.

◆ Most people in the Rhineland welcomed their reunion with Germany.

◆ Britain and France did nothing to oppose Germany's actions beyond verbal protests.

◆ Some people in Britain were alarmed by the reoccupation, but many others took the view that Germany was only reclaiming territory which was rightfully hers, and regarded it as resolving a problem created at Versailles.

Evaluating Visual Sources

You should go through the same kind of process if you are asked a similar question based on a photograph. Take a look at this one:

Example

Source Y: This is a photograph of a poster on a house in Vienna, March 1938. The poster reads, 'Common Blood belongs together in one Reich'.

Assess the value of Source Y as evidence of attitudes in Austria towards the Anschluss of 1938.

(5 marks)

Although there is less detailed evidence for you to find in this photograph than in Shepard's cartoon, there is still enough to write a good answer. You could refer first of all to the origin of the source, which is a contemporary photograph taken in Vienna, the Austrian capital, in the month of the Anschluss. Assessing its purpose is a bit speculative, but it might be propaganda to demonstrate Austrian support for the union with Germany.

You could point out that this illustrates the views of those Austrians who supported the Anschluss, as the poster refers to the argument that Austrians and Germans were of the same 'blood', meaning that they were closely related. The photograph also shows a march of what appear to be people in a costume that is not a military uniform, behind a flag that looks like the Austrian flag with a swastika, the Nazi symbol. This may indicate support by Austrian people for the Anschluss.

From recall, you could note that many Austrians did support the Anschluss. This was shown by the welcome received by German troops and Hitler himself when he entered Vienna, and by the very high 'yes' vote in the plebiscite that followed (though results of such votes under the Nazis are always slightly dubious as many were frightened to vote against). On the other hand, there were Austrians who were less happy with the union, especially once the Nazis began to humiliate Jewish people in public, and you may wish to illustrate this by noting that Hitler occupied Austria to prevent Chancellor Schuschnigg from holding his own vote, where it was expected that they would reject the union with Germany.

Having made some of these points, you should then answer the question in a brief conclusion, perhaps arguing that this source is good evidence that a substantial number of Austrians welcomed the Anschluss, but that there were also those who held opposite views.

Here is an example from another Special Topic, *The Origins and Development of the Cold War 1945–1985*.

Example

Source Z: Aerial reconnaissance photograph of San Cristobol, Cuba, October 1962.

How valuable is **Source Z** in explaining the reasons for the United States' policy during the Cuban crisis of 1962?   (5 marks)

While this is obviously a primary source, what makes this particularly important in explaining United States policy on Cuba is that it is an intelligence photograph used by the USA both to inform and to justify its policy during the crisis. It gives clear evidence that the Soviet Union was placing missiles in Cuba that were capable of striking the United States. You could illustrate this by referring to the labels indicating storage areas and launch areas for missiles.

Your recall could include information about the state of the arms race in 1962, but note that the missiles in Cuba were especially worrying to the Americans as they were so close to the USA that they provoked fears of a surprise attack, which could be launched with little or no warning, giving the USA no time to make a counter-attack. This was what made President Kennedy so determined to force the Soviet Union to remove the missiles, leading to his decision to blockade Cuba.

Your conclusion could be that this source is extremely valuable in explaining the reasons for the United States policy at the time of the Cuban crisis as it was a key piece of evidence in influencing Kennedy's decision to act at a time when tension between East and West was already high.

Comparing sources

A source comparison question can be written in several ways, but what you have to do to answer them stays the same. Here are some examples:

- *How far do Sources X and Y agree about …?*
- *To what extent do Sources X and Y differ about …?*
- *Compare the views in Sources X and Y about …*
- *To what extent does the evidence in Source X support the views expressed in Source Y?*

This time the prompt beneath will always ask you to:

- *Compare the sources overall and in detail.*

The most common mistake people make in answering this kind of question is to think they are actually comparing sources when they are really only making lists of points. They write something like:

> Source X says … list of points, often copied word for word from the source.
>
> Source Y says … another list, just like the last
>
> Therefore the sources agree – or disagree.

This is a very poor answer, because there has been no attempt to compare anything that the sources said, and because the copying fails to show any real understanding of what either of them said.

Remember

Good answers to source comparison questions will prove that you understand the main argument of each source – the overall comparison. Do the authors agree about the issue or not? (In most cases they will disagree at least on some points, though maybe not on everything.) As with the source evaluations, you need to *prove* your statement that they agree or disagree by comparing specific points from the sources – what made you *think* they had the same or different views.

It is worth noting that answers to source comparison questions can be awarded full marks without having any recalled knowledge. However, if you think that some recalled knowledge will help to explain a point of difference, you may put it in your answer and, if it does help in this way, it can be given credit. There is also no need to comment on the origins and purpose of either source, unless for some reason it helps you to explain the comparison more effectively.

Here are two sources from the 2003 examination. The issue to which they refer is the Anschluss between Austria and Germany.

Example

Source B: from an article in the *Daily Worker*, the newspaper of the British Communist Party, 12 March 1938.

> British people must act. The struggle for British peace and democracy has entered a stage of great tension. In Spain, Franco has launched his offensive. In Austria the great majority of people are heroically fighting for their independence. At the time of writing German troops are sitting on the Austrian border … When are British people going to pull their weight in this historic struggle? Chamberlain has declared that small nations in Europe need not look to the League of Nations. This is a plain indication to Hitler that so far as Britain is concerned he is free to destroy the independence of Austria and Czechoslovakia.
>
> The British people should be under no illusions. If fascism wins in these countries it will threaten the very existence of democracy in Britain. It is not merely the peace of central Europe that is trembling in the balance. It is the peace of the world.

Example continued ➤

Example *continued*

Source C: from a speech by Lord Londonderry in the House of Lords, 16 March 1938.

It is no good disguising from ourselves that what has happened in Austria was a foregone conclusion. We can see by the enthusiasm with which Hitler is regarded in Austria that his arrival is welcomed by the great majority of the population.

This change has relieved the terrible tension that has existed in Austria for many years. The great majority of the Austrian population are in favour of the change that has come about. Chancellor Schuschnigg, instead of making a peaceful declaration, has made the situation more dangerous. I think that had the plebiscite taken place it would have been followed by riots, bloodshed and Communist revolution, and we might have seen in Austria the same circumstances as we see in Spain at the present moment. One must feel that drastic action by Herr Hitler has prevented bloodshed and revolution.

Compare the views of **Sources B** and **C** concerning the Anschluss in Austria in March 1938.

(5 marks)

Compare the sources overall and in detail.

I'll do the comparison as a table, to let you see the direct points of contrast, though of course this is not acceptable in the examination. Your answer should make the same kinds of points, but written normally in paragraphs.

Source B	Source C
Overall view is hostile to the Anschluss, as might be expected of a Communist source.	Overall view is sympathetic to the Anschluss.
Demands that the British take action.	The Anschluss was inevitable.
British democracy is under threat from fascism in Spain and in Austria.	The threat to peace is from Communist revolution which would have created the same problems in Austria as in Spain.
'The great majority of people' in Austria are fighting to defend their independence from Germany.	'The great majority of the Austrian population' welcome Hitler with enthusiasm and support the Anschluss.
Writer is critical of Chamberlain for failing to protect small countries against aggression.	Writer is critical of Schuschnigg for making the situation dangerous instead of accepting the union with Germany peacefully.
What is happening in Spain and Austria is threatening the peace of the world	By uniting Germany and Austria Hitler has prevented the riots and bloodshed that would have been caused by a plebiscite.

An answer that contained all, or probably even most, of these points, making the direct comparisons between them, would have gained full marks.

Summary

In answering a source comparison question:

1   **Identify the main argument in each source and whether they agree or disagree.**

2   **Support your overall comparison by balancing points of detail from each source, pointing out any agreements or disagreements.**

3   **Give a short conclusion that answers the question.**

For Practice

Task 2

Here are three pairs of sources, from different Historical Special Topics. As this exercise deals with source comparisons, and all the information you need is in the sources, try this with all three Special Topics. For each pair of sources:

◆   identify the view of the author of each source towards the issue in the question,

◆   list three specific points of comparison between the sources.

Scotland 1689–1715

Source A: from an address to the Scottish Parliament by the General Convention of Royal Burghs, 29 October 1706.

By an incorporating Union, our monarchy is suppressed, our Parliaments destroyed. As a result our religion, Church government, Claim of Right, laws, liberties and trade and all that is dear to us is daily in danger of being interfered with, altered or completely undermined by the English. In a British Parliament, the poor representation allowed for Scotland can never secure our interest.

And by these articles our poor people are made liable to the English taxes, which is a certain insupportable burden. The trade proposed is uncertain, and wholly precarious … The most considerable branches of our trade differ from those of the English, and may be yet more discouraged by them.

Source B: from a speech in Parliament in the debate on the Treaty of Union by William Seton of Pitmedden, 1706.

I could give some account of the particular advantages we'll obtain by an incorporating Union with England. In general, I may assert, that by this Union we'll have access to all the advantages of commerce the English enjoy. We'll be able to improve our national product for the benefit of the whole island. We'll have our liberty, property and religion secured under the protection of one sovereign and one Parliament of Great Britain.

Compare the views in **Sources A and B** on the effects on Scotland of an incorporating Union with England. (5 marks)

For Practice continued ➤

For Practice *continued*

Patterns of Migration: Scotland 1830s–1930s

Source A: from the evidence given by Bishop Andrew Scott in the *Report of the State of the Irish Poor in Great Britain*, 1836.

A considerable number of . . . immoral characters immigrate from Ireland to this country . . . The conduct of these people, who from their crimes become best known, is considered by many a part of their national character, and the whole body of the Irish migrants are reproached with their crimes. These reproaches irritate their minds, and tend to keep up a spirit of animosity between them and the natives . . . Groundless prejudices against the whole of them exist to a great degree, even among the respectable classes of society. Their naturally warm temper is generally kept in a state of strong agitation, from the continual taunts thrown out by the natives against their country and against their religion, and on ignorant minds this must naturally produce a very bad effect.

Source B: from evidence given by a mill owner in Blairgowrie, *Fourth Report on Intemperance*, 1878.

We have a large Irish Roman Catholic population in Blairgowrie . . . They are first-rate workers, and are very well conducted in every way, and the reason is simply this, that the Roman Catholic priest is a man of superior character, a first-rate man. He has for the last twenty years devoted himself night and day to the improvement of his people. He has built a fine school and passed, I think, 98 per cent of his scholars, and even some of the little girls are wonderfully good scholars.

Compare the attitudes towards Irish immigrants to Scotland revealed in **Sources A and B**.

(5 marks)

Appeasement and the Road to War, to 1939

Source A: from a press release by Winston Churchill MP, 21 September 1938.

The partition of Czechoslovakia under pressure from England and France amounts to the complete surrender of the Western Democracies to the Nazi threat of force. Such a collapse will bring peace or security neither to England nor to France. On the contrary, it will place these two nations in an ever weaker and more dangerous situation. The mere neutralisation of Czechoslovakia means the liberation of twenty-five German divisions, which will threaten the Western front . . . It is not Czechoslovakia alone which is menaced, but also the freedom and the democracy of all nations.

Source B: from a leading article in the *Kilmarnock Standard*, 5 October 1938.

The Prime Minister by the Munich agreement has achieved a great success for pacific diplomacy as against threats of violence. It is true that there has been a considerable amount of criticism . . . but on the whole the weight of sober opinion remains largely in Mr Chamberlain's favour. The Sudeten Germans . . . have never been able to reconcile themselves to Czech rule . . . and therefore it must be admitted that there was a racial

For Practice *continued* ➤

For Practice *continued*

grievance to be remedied. The Prime Minister has been able to secure a lasting settlement of this controversy without bloodshed. Whatever we may think of Herr Hitler's methods . . . the fact remains that the Sudeten Germans . . . wanted union with Germany. And that being so, the only practical course to take was that which Mr Chamberlain adopted.

To what extent do **Sources A and B** differ in their attitudes towards the Czech crisis of 1938? (5 marks)

You can compare your answers with mine on pages 102–103.

Placing sources in their historical context

The final skill you have to demonstrate in the examination is to 'relate sources accurately to historical developments and events through recall'. Various phrasings are used in questions like this, but they all have the same purpose – to test whether you can link the evidence from the source or sources to your knowledge of the period you are studying. Most questions of this kind will be worth 5 or 6 marks, except that there will be one question like this based on three sources, and this one will be for 8 marks.

Questions testing this skill can take several forms. For instance:

- *How fully does Source X show/illustrate/ explain …?*
- *How far/to what extent do you accept/agree with the views in Source X about … ?*
- *How typical is Source X of views at the time about … ?*
- *How accurate is the description/explanation in Source X about …?*
- *How far/to what extent does Source X reflect/show/illustrate/explain …?*
- *Is there enough evidence in Source X to argue that … ?*

Or there may be a question followed by the instruction to refer to Source X and your recalled knowledge.

All questions of this type are now followed by the prompt:

- *Use the source and recalled knowledge.*

Although you may be asked to assess a primary source in this way, this kind of question can refer as easily to a secondary source, asking you to evaluate an historian's interpretation of an issue rather than a contemporary observer's view. You should not assume that you must agree with the historian just because he or she is a professional and has probably studied the topic in more depth than you have. The historian's opinions may be based on deeper study than yours, but so are the opinions of all the other historians who have reached different conclusions by interpreting the evidence in different ways. What matters is not whether you agree with the historian but whether you can argue your case sensibly by reference to appropriate evidence.

Whether the source is primary or secondary, there are two stages in answering a question of this kind. First, as with the source evaluation questions, you need to work out what the source is saying: what is its overall view and what detailed points of content told you that? Here is an example of a source and possible question from the Special Topic, *The Origins and Development of the Cold War*.

Example

Source A: from an article in *Pravda*, 23 November 1956, quoted by the United Nations 'Report of the Special Committee on the Problem of Hungary', January 1957.

> A Socialist state could not remain an indifferent observer of the bloody reign of Fascist reaction in People's Democratic Hungary. When everything settles down in Hungary, and life becomes normal again, the Hungarian working class, peasantry and intelligentsia will undoubtedly understand our actions better and judge them as right. We regard the help to the Hungarian working class in its struggle against the intrigues of counter-revolution as our international duty.

To what extent do you accept the explanation in **Source A** of the invasion of Hungary by Warsaw Pact forces in 1956? (6 marks)

Use the source and recalled knowledge.

Although in most cases it is not necessary in answering questions of this kind to refer to the provenance of the source, here it makes some sense to do so, because it is so obviously presenting the Soviet point of view. Having noted this bias, you could comment on the *overall* point of view by saying that the source claims that the invasion was to help the people of Hungary resist fascism and counter-revolution. Points of *detail* to explain this interpretation could include the allegation that the Hungarian government had been using violence against its people ('bloody reign'), the hope that the Hungarian people – it refers to three classes of people – would understand the intervention in time, and the statement that the Soviet Union saw it as its duty to defend the Hungarian working class.

Stage two in answering the question is to compare the claims of the source with your recalled knowledge, to support an evaluation of whether you agree or disagree with the source. Here, there are many points of recall that you could use. It is much easier to disagree with the source than to agree with it, because the evidence from the time showed that the Hungarian people resisted the Soviet troops, who were forced to use tanks on the streets of Budapest. The reforms by the Hungarian government that provoked the Warsaw Pact invasion were popular with most Hungarians, and the true reason for the invasion was the fear in the Soviet Union that if reform went ahead in Hungary, it might undermine the whole Soviet system in eastern Europe. It is important that you try to link points of recall to the judgement you make, so that you actually give reasons to support your evaluation.

That question asked you to use evidence to *agree* or *disagree* with the source. Just as often you will use your knowledge to show that the source does not explain the whole story. The clue that the examiners *want* you to do this comes in phrases like 'To what extent …' or 'How far …' does the source explain a particular issue. Here is an example from *Appeasement and the Road to War, to 1939* from the 2004 examination paper. In this case the source is a cartoon from the magazine *Punch*, published in September 1938 during Chamberlain's efforts to deal with the crisis over the Sudetenland.

Example

To what extent does the cartoon illustrate Chamberlain's policy during the Czech crisis of 1938? (6 marks)

Use the source and recalled knowledge.

So the first thing to do is to see how the cartoonist interprets Chamberlain's efforts. For once, here is a cartoonist who seems to support Chamberlain (the overall view), because he is shown as working to save the world from war. Points of detail to support this interpretation could include:

◆ Chamberlain is shown working hard, with his sleeves rolled up, to push the world across the plank of the Czech crisis, away from Chaos and towards peace.

◆ The cartoonist sees this as a difficult and dangerous task, as shown by the crack in the plank and stones falling away from both sides of the chasm.

◆ If Chamberlain were to fail, the consequences would be to send the world falling onto the sharp rocks of war beneath.

You can judge the extent to which this shows Chamberlain's policy by considering what he actually did and said at the time. He certainly said that he was determined to avoid war if he could, and made no less than three trips to Germany by air in just over two weeks to negotiate with Hitler. Given when the cartoon was published, the cartoonist almost certainly had at least one of these trips in mind. The evaluation of Chamberlain's policy can be argued either way: by the end of September the Munich agreement postponed war so it can be argued to have been successful; but many people at the time and since have seen that agreement as giving in to aggression, and, of course, war did break out less than a year later. You could make some of these points before reaching a conclusion that answers the question, perhaps pointing out that while the source *does* show Chamberlain working for peace it does *not* deal with the feelings of the Czech people or show the reasons for Chamberlain's efforts.

A visual source can also be used as the basis for other ways of placing sources in their historical context:

Example

Source P: *The Train Robbery*, a cartoon in *Punch*, 18 January 1967.

The Train Robbery

How accurately does **Source P** illustrate the effects on the United States of involvement in the Vietnam War?   (6 marks)

In this case, there is little point in discussing the provenance of the source, as you are not being asked to comment on its value as evidence. You would do much better to concentrate on the message of the cartoon. The cartoonist shows the American economy as a train, pulling trucks representing the 'Great Society'. However, the Great Society is being broken up as fuel for the Vietnam War, shown as the smoke from the funnel of the train. The person swinging the axe that is breaking up the trucks is President Lyndon Johnson. So how accurate is this picture of Johnson's involvement in Vietnam destroying the US economy and society?

Among the evidence from recall that you could use to comment on this might be:

◆ The United States' involvement in Vietnam was not, at first, expected or intended to involve US troops in fighting, but by 1967 the United States had been dragged deeper and deeper into the conflict by the inability of the South Vietnamese forces to resist the Vietcong. This led to a massive drain on American resources, as illustrated in the cartoon.

◆ By 1967, the war was causing huge splits in American society, as people found it hard to accept that the most powerful country in the world was failing to defeat a third world guerrilla army. This was made worse by the rising casualty figures and by terrible images on television news, which appalled many Americans.

◆ These feelings were shown by an active anti-war campaign involving a wide range of people including sportsmen like Muhammad Ali, people from the world of entertainment such as Pete Seeger and Bob Dylan, and the great civil rights leader Martin Luther King. On the other hand, conservative politicans and ex-servicemen often supported the war and argued that opposing the war was letting down the soldiers.

It could, therefore, be argued that the cartoon is accurate both in showing the impact of Vietnam on the American economy and in its view that the war was damaging American society, ruining the 'American Dream'.

Example

Although visual, sometimes a source may also have important text. In the 2001 examination, in the Special Topic *Ireland 1900–1985: A Divided Identity*, **Source A** was this Unionist poster from 1912:

ULSTER PROVISIONAL GOVERNMENT PROCLAMATION

TO ALL WHOM IT MAY CONCERN

Whereas Ulstermen, Free Citizens of a United Kingdom, Born into Possession of Full Rights and Privileges under ONE KING AND ONE IMPERIAL PARLIAMENT, are threatened with the calamity of being deprived of their Birthright and being Forcibly subjected to a Nationalist Parliament and Executive, regardless of their steadfast allegiance in the past to their King and Empire.

BE IT KNOWN

That for the Public Safety and Security of Civil and Religious Liberty to ALL Classes and Creeds, duly elected Delegates and Covenanters representative of all parts of Ulster in the City of Belfast this day assembled finally settled the form of

PROVISIONAL GOVERNMENT

WITHIN THE PROVINCE OF ULSTER

THE DATE upon which it shall become effective together with instructions regarding all other matters necessary for Repudiating and Resisting the Decrees of such Nationalist Parliament or Executive and for taking over the Government of the Province IN TRUST for the British Nation will be made public as and when it shall be deemed expedient.

ON BEHALF OF THE CENTRAL AUTHORITY

EDWARD CARSON
LONDONDERRY
ABERCORN
JOHN YOUNG
THOMAS SINCLAIR
THOMAS ANDREWS

OLD TOWN HALL, BELFAST, 24TH SEPTEMBER, 1912

GOD SAVE THE KING

To what extent were the views expressed in **Source A** influenced by events and developments in Ireland in the years up to 1912?

(6 marks)

Multi-source Questions

Here, to set the source in context, you need to identify the views in the source and then use your recalled knowledge to show your understanding of the ways in which events in the previous years had led to such strong feelings among the Unionist community.

The poster was a statement signed by several prominent Unionists, including Sir Edward Carson, that, if Britain tried to enforce Home Rule on Ireland, they would set up a Provisional Government for Ulster. The poster proclaimed the Unionists' fear that Home Rule would force Ulster to be subjected to Nationalist (by which they meant Roman Catholic) rule. It also identified the reasons, setting up a Provisional Government as the defence of public safety and the security of civil and religious freedom.

So, what recalled knowledge could you use to comment on the growth of these views in Ulster? For one thing, Ulster was the only province of Ireland with a Protestant majority, so it was not surprising that they were afraid that any government for the whole of Ireland would pass laws to suit Roman Catholics. Second, the economy of Ulster was different from the rest of Ireland, being based on industry rather than agriculture, so the Unionists feared that economic policy in an independent Ireland would damage their prosperity. However, both of these had been true for many years, but it was only in the years leading up to 1912 that the Liberal Government's dependence on Irish Members of Parliament had led to the prospect of a Home Rule Bill being passed. It was the growing likelihood of this that had led to increased tension in Ulster, leading to the signing of the Ulster Covenant and to the proclamation on the poster.

Your conclusion might argue, then, that in part these views had developed over a long period, with Protestant and Unionist nervousness about their possible loss of status and power and concerns over how they would be treated in a Roman Catholic state. However, it was the fact that Home Rule now appeared imminent that led to such extreme actions as those outlined in the source.

The Three Source Question

A special case of this kind of question is the three-source question. Often, two of the sources will be primary sources with the third being an historian's comment on the issue. These questions fall into two kinds:

◆ A question asking how far the three sources explain an issue. In these cases the sources usually give you some of the factors or reasons, but omit some, so giving you a chance to fill in the gaps from recalled knowledge.

◆ A broad question that asks you to refer to three sources and recalled knowledge. Often the three sources will take different views on the issue, so you should supply recalled knowledge to support your agreement with one or other of their points of view.

Example

Some recent questions for eight marks have been:

The Crusades
To what extent were both rich and poor crusaders motivated by spiritual reward rather than material gain? Refer to Sources A, C and D in your answer. (2002) – second type

Scotland 1689–1715
How adequately do Sources B, C and D explain the motives of the Scottish parliament in accepting the treaty of Union? (2004) – first type

The American Revolution
To what extent do Sources B, C and D explain the reasons for British defeat in the War of Independence? (2000) – first type

Patterns of Migration: Scotland 1830s–1930s
How successfully did Irish immigrants assimilate into Scottish society during the period 1830s–1930s? Refer to Sources B, C and D and recalled knowledge. (2002) – second type

Appeasement and the Road to War, to 1939
How fully do Sources A, C and E identify the issues in Europe which led to war in 1939? (2001) – first type

The Origins and Development of the Cold War 1945–1985
How important was ideology in the development of international tension during the Cold War? Use Sources B, C and E and recalled knowledge. (2004) – second type

Ireland 1900–1985: A Divided Identity
Why did it prove so difficult to resolve the issues causing tension in Ireland between 1912 and 1921? Refer to Sources A, C and D and your own knowledge. (2000) – second type

The most successful answers to this kind of question are written as short essays. A short introduction lets you show that you understand the issue and identify some of the possible factors. For example, an answer to the question about the reasons for the outbreak of war in 1939 could begin something like this:

> The Second World War broke out in September 1939 as a climax to years of international tension. This tension resulted from the rise to power of Fascist governments who were willing to challenge the settlement of 1919 and from the difficulties facing democratic governments in responding to this challenge.

The answer could then look at specific reasons mentioned in the three sources named in the question. These sources were:

♦ a cartoon from the *Scottish Daily Express* in 1936 showing a soldier wearing jackboots marching into the Rhineland over a table at which politicians are saying that the League of Nations would never allow it

♦ a letter to the editor of the *Scotsman* in 1936 protesting at the failure of British and other democracies to defend the elected government in Spain against aggression supported by Germany and Italy

♦ an historian's analysis showing how the Spanish Civil War had become a battleground between Fascism and Communism, criticising British governments for being unprepared at each of the crises between 1936 and 1938 and commenting on Chamberlain's ambition to have one great settlement of Europe's diplomatic problems.

Your answer could point out that the sources do identify several issues that made war possible in Europe: Fascist aggression, the weakness of democratic governments to resist and the failure of the League of Nations both encouraging further aggression. However, they do not mention all of the issues, so you could bring in some of these from recall, perhaps including the lack of trust of the Soviet Union among the British and French, the frantic rearmament of the two or three years before 1939, and the eventual abandonment of appeasement and determination to resist any further attacks.

The good answer then finishes with a conclusion that sums up your opinion on the issue. For example:

The sources do identify a number of the reasons that led to war, including German aggression over the Rhineland and in Spain, the failure of the League of Nations and of democratic countries to resist Hitler in time, and Chamberlain's willingness to appease Germany in search of a 'general settlement' of Europe that was never possible outside his own imagination. However, they omit factors that weakened the democratic countries and made them unable to resist in a way that might have prevented war by checking Hitler earlier. These included lack of trust between Britain and France, economic problems that held back military spending in the early 1930s and public opinion that would not have permitted military action before 1938 at the earliest.

EVALUATING SOURCES

Summary

In answers to questions that ask you to place sources in context:

1   Identify the issue raised by the question.

2   Extract relevant evidence from the source or sources.

3   Comment on their accuracy or completeness by using evidence from recall.

4   Write a short conclusion that sums up what you have said and answers the question.

For Practice

Task 3

Look at these sources and the questions beneath them. For the Special Topic you are studying:

◆   explain the overall opinion of the author towards the issue raised in the question

◆   give two points of detail from the source that support your interpretation

◆   give two points of recalled knowledge that you could use to comment on the source.

You can then compare your ideas with mine on pages 103–105.

The Crusades 1096–1204 (from the 2003 examination)
Source C: from A. Maalouf, *The Crusades through Arab Eyes* (1983).

> The strong man of Cairo, vizier al-Afdal, had not concealed his satisfaction when, in April 1097, ambassadors from Alexius Comnenus had informed him that a massive contingent of Frankish knights had arrived in Constantinople and were about to launch an offensive in Asia Minor.

For Practice continued ➤

For Practice continued

Since the middle of the century, Seljuk advances had been eroding the territory of the Fatimid caliphate and the Byzantine Empire alike. Al-Afdal dreamed of a concerted operation by the two allied powers, and when he learned that the emperor had received a large reinforcement of troops from the lands of the Franks, he felt that revenge was at hand.

The delegation he dispatched to the besiegers at Antioch made no mention of a non-aggression pact. That much was obvious, thought the vizier. What he proposed to the Franks was a formal partition, northern Syria for the Franks, southern Syria (meaning Palestine, Damascus and the coastal cities as far north as Beirut) for him.

How fully does Maalouf (**Source C**) illustrate the weaknesses of the Muslims during the First Crusade? (6 marks)

Use the source and recalled knowledge.

The American Revolution (from the 2004 examination)
Source D: from a letter from George Washington to Joseph Reed, May 1780.

We ought not to deceive ourselves. The naval resources of Great Britain are more substantial than those of France and Spain united. Her commerce is more extensive than that of both her rivals … In modern wars the largest purse must chiefly determine the event. I fear that our enemy will be found to have the largest purse. I have no doubt that ample means will be found to prosecute the war with the greatest vigour.

France is in a very different position … If the war continues for another campaign France will be obliged to impose the taxes usual in time of war which are very heavy, and which the people of France are not in a position to endure for any duration. When this necessity commences France makes war on ruinous terms; and England will find it much easier to supply her needs.

How accurate is Washington's assessment in **Source D** of British advantages in the American War of Independence? (6 marks)

Use the source and recalled knowledge.

Appeasement and the Road to War, to 1939
Source X: from a memorandum to the Cabinet by Anthony Eden, the Foreign Secretary, January 1937.

The Spanish Civil War has ceased to be an internal Spanish issue and has become an international battleground. The character of the future government of Spain has become less important to the peace of Europe than that the dictators should not be victorious in that country . . .

It is therefore my conviction that unless we cry a halt in Spain, we shall have trouble this year . . . It follows that to be firm in Spain is to gain time, and to gain time is what we want.

For Practice continued ➤

For Practice continued

How far do you accept Eden's assessment in **Source X** of the international importance of the Spanish Civil War? (6 marks)

Use the source and recalled knowledge.

The Origins and Development of the Cold War

Source Y: from a message, Nikita Khrushchev to President John F. Kennedy, 27 October 1962.

You want to make your country safe. This is understandable; but Cuba too wants the same thing. All countries want to make themselves safe.

But how are we, the Soviet Union, to assess your actions, which are expressed in the fact that you have surrounded with military bases the Soviet Union, surrounded with military bases our allies; have disposed military bases literally around our country; have stationed your rocket armament there?

Your rockets are situated in Italy, and are aimed at us. Your rockets are situated in Turkey. You are worried by Cuba. You say it worries you because it is a distance of 90 miles by sea from the coast of America.

But Turkey is next to us. Our sentries walk up and down and look at each other.

How justified was Khrushchev's assessment of the Cuban crisis in **Source Y**? (6 marks)

Use the source and recalled knowledge.

Ireland 1900–1985: A Divided Identity

Source Z: from a speech by John Dillon MP in the House of Commons in a debate following the collapse of the Easter Rising in 1916.

I know they were wrong, but they fought a clean fight, and they fought with superb bravery and skill, and no act of savagery has been blamed on any leader or any organized body of insurgents . . .

As a matter of fact the great bulk of the population were not favourable to the insurrection. The insurgents themselves, who had confidently counted on a rising of the people in their support, were absolutely disappointed. They got no popular support whatever. What is happening is that thousands of people in Dublin, who ten days ago were bitterly opposed to the whole of the Sinn Féin movement and to the rebellion, are now becoming infuriated against the Government on account of these executions. I am now informed, by letters received this morning, that feeling is spreading throughout the country in a most dangerous degree.

To what extent does **Source Z** explain the increase in support for Sinn Féin between 1916 and 1918? (6 marks)

Use the source and recalled knowledge.

SOLUTIONS TO TASKS

Task 1

The Crusades

Overall view: the crusades were called in response to the Muslim mistreatment of Christian places in the Holy Land.

Detail from the source:

◆ describes the invaders as barbarians

◆ the invaders have taken Jerusalem, the city where Christ died

◆ churches have been raided.

Points from recall:

◆ the letter is written by the Pope who called the crusade, so reflects his view

◆ there were other influences on the calling of the crusade, such as the appeal for help from Constantinople.

The American Revolution

Overall view: argues that if the Americans want British protection they must accept the laws and taxes passed by the British parliament.

Detail from the source:

◆ the source says that the Americans cannot just refuse to accept the Stamp Act

◆ if the colonies are not British possessions, parliament does not rule them at all and has no duty to protect them

◆ if they are British, they must accept all laws of Parliament.

Points from recall:

◆ this was the argument of those who wanted to pressurise the Americans into doing what Parliament said

◆ other British people were more sympathetic towards the American claim that they should not be taxed in this way without some say in the passing of the law – 'No taxation without representation'.

Appeasement and the Road to War, to 1939

Overall view: the writer accepts the Anschluss as desirable and in the interests of Austria.

Detail from the source:

◆ there has been no violent opposition to the Anschluss in Austria, therefore the people in general welcomed it

◆ Anschluss would have happened earlier but for unreasonable opposition from the European powers

◆ the outcome will be good economically for Austria and will prevent future trouble.

Points from recall:

◆ this was a common view at the time among people who were pro-appeasement or anti-Communist

◆ by this stage there was a growing minority of people who supported Churchill's line that the Anschluss was evidence of German ambition and would open the way for Hitler to attack Czechoslovakia and other eastern European countries.

Task 2

Scotland 1689–1715

Overall views

A: strongly against an incorporating Union, which would be damaging for Scotland.

B: in favour of an incorporating Union, which would be of benefit to Scotland.

Detailed comparison

A	B
Incorporating Union would take away the Scottish monarchy and Parliament.	It would be better for Scotland to be under the protection of one monarch and Parliament for Great Britain
Scottish religion, law and freedoms would be damaged.	Union would protect Scottish laws, freedoms and religion.
Union would impose English taxes on Scotland with no certainty of better trade through the Union.	Scotland would benefit from sharing in trade with English colonies, so the economy would improve.

Patterns of Migration 1830s–1930s

Overall views

A: very negative attitude towards Irish immigrants to Scotland, who have not fitted well into Scottish society.

B: positive view of the Irish, who have contributed well to the town.

Detailed comparison

A	B
Many Irish immigrants are immoral and this causes trouble between them and the Scots.	Irish workers in Blairgowrie are hard working and well-behaved.
Many Irish are quick-tempered and ignorant.	The Roman Catholic priest is a good influence and has helped to educate the young immigrants.
Many Scots are prejudiced against the Irish, and this leads to animosity between the two groups.	Though there is no direct statement in the source about this issue, the language of praise used throughout shows no anti-Irish feeling.

Appeasement and the Road to War, to 1939

Overall views

A: strongly anti-appeasement and against any deal with Hitler giving him part of Czechoslovakia.

B: pro-appeasement, regarding the Munich agreement as the only reasonable solution.

Detailed comparison:

A	B
Western democratic countries are giving in to Hitler's threat to use force.	Munich agreement is a success for diplomacy over violence.
Breaking up Czechoslovakia would not bring peace, but would increase the threat to Britain and France.	Chamberlain has managed to resolve the crisis without shedding blood – that is, peacefully
To give Hitler what he wants would only strengthen Germany and threaten the peace of everyone.	The agreement has solved a real grievance and was the only practical way to do so.

Task 3

The Crusades 1096–1204

Overall view: a main reason for Muslim weakness was the willingness of the Muslim leader Al-Afdal to become an ally of the crusaders against other Muslims.

Detailed points:

◆ Al-Afdal was a rival of the Seljuks who had been taking territory from him.

◆ He approached the Frankish crusaders with a proposal to split Syria with them.

From recall:

◆ There were religious divisions between Sunni Muslims, led from Baghdad and Shia Muslims, led from Cairo.

◆ The Muslims had military disadvantages when faced with the armoured knights of the crusaders.

The American Revolution

Overall view: the main British advantage was its economic and naval strength, both of which were greater than those of the Americans' European allies.

Detailed points:

◆ In modern war the richest usually win, and Britain has better trade and a better navy than either France or Spain.

◆ If the war carries on, France will have to tax its people, who cannot afford to pay, therefore France will be in a weak position.

From recall:

◆ British wealth also allowed her to pay mercenary soldiers from some German states.

◆ Though Washington's argument was accurate in theory, the French navy actually made a decisive contribution towards the end of the war. In any case, these advantages were outweighed by the difficulties of fighting a war 3,000 miles from Britain against a determined local population.

Appeasement and the Road to War, to 1939

Overall view: Britain should intervene in the Spanish Civil War to prevent a fascist victory.

Detailed points:

◆ The issue in Spain is now an international one of preventing victory for the dictators.

◆ Britain should act firmly to gain time before the outbreak of any further trouble.

From recall:

◆ Eden was right that Spain was now an international issue, with Hitler and Mussolini supporting Franco, Stalin and the International Brigades supporting the Republicans.

◆ Hitler used Spain as a testing ground for German troops and for the Luftwaffe, so helping his military build-up. This helped Hitler to prepare to make more aggressive demands such as in Austria and Czechoslovakia not much more than a year later.

The Origins and Development of the Cold War

Overall view: the placing of Soviet missiles in Cuba was no worse and possibly less threatening than the placement of American missiles such as those in Italy and Turkey.

Detailed points:

◆ Khrushchev understands the wish of the USA to be safe, but this applies to all countries.

◆ The USA has surrounded the Soviet Union and its allies with military bases and rockets, those in Turkey being right on the Soviet border.

From recall:

◆ The crisis resulted from placing of Soviet missiles in Cuba, and was resolved by Khrushchev's decision to order ships carrying missiles to turn back, causing him loss of prestige in the USSR.

◆ Khrushchev's point about US forces and missiles was accurate, but does not take into account that these were a response to perceived threats by the Soviet Union against western Europe through the size of Warsaw Pact forces in places like East Germany.

Ireland 1900–1985: A Divided Identity

Overall view: the reaction of the British government to the Easter Rising has turned opinion in Ireland in favour of Sinn Féin.

Detailed points:

◆ Until the execution of leaders of the Rising, most Irish people were against the rebels, as was shown by the fact that the people of Dublin did not rise to support them.

◆ Dillon has received letters that have convinced him of the level of anger in Ireland about the executions.

From recall:

◆ Dillon was correct that many Irishmen were disgusted at the treatment of the prisoners, whom they regarded as not very important. By executing them, the British turned them into martyrs and stimulated support for the nationalist cause.

◆ The other main reason for rising support for Sinn Féin was the introduction of conscription in Ireland. By 1918 Sinn Féin was strong enough to win the General Election in Ireland.

SECTION 3

Sample Essays

Chapter 9

COMMENTARIES ON SAMPLE ESSAYS

Introduction

In this section you will find some examples of real essays written by pupils in Scottish schools, with commentaries on their strengths and weaknesses, together with an indication of the mark that the essay would have been awarded had it been written in the examination. After a few general points, each essay will be discussed under five headings. Each will contain remarks addressing several questions outlined below.

Structure

◆ Is the essay well organised into paragraphs?

◆ Is the approach mainly narrative or descriptive, or does it show qualities of analysis and evaluation?

Introduction

◆ Is there a recognisable introduction?

◆ Does it show that the writer understands what the question asks her/him to **do**?

◆ Does it give some clues as to how the writer will approach the rest of the essay?

Evidence

◆ Is there an appropriate amount of relevant factual information?

◆ Is it accurate?

◆ Is there a lot of irrelevant material?

◆ Is the evidence **used** to support or develop a line of argument, or is it simply presented to show off some recalled knowledge?

◆ Does the writer show awareness of alternative interpretations, or of historical debate?

Conclusion

◆ Is there a recognisable conclusion?

◆ Does it just repeat points made earlier, or does it summarise an argument?

◆ Does it **answer the question**?

Overall

◆ Taking into account the strengths and weaknesses, what would the essay be worth in the external examination?

Essay 1

How far was Britain democratic by 1918?

'The best argument against democracy is a five-minute conversation with the average voter'. – Winston Churchill

Our views on what exactly a democracy is are not fixed and will probably continue to evolve, but it is generally agreed that a democracy should include universality of voting, a corruption-free system, free choice and secrecy. Before 1832 Britain was not democratic at all, and few measures were in place to change this. From 1832 onwards, however, changes were gradually made to make the government more effective and to move Britain towards becoming a democracy. By examining the extent of the franchise, voting procedures, popular involvement and the share of power, it can be seen how democratic Britain had become by 1918.

Before 1832 very few people had the vote. In 1832 the Great Reform Act increased the franchise so that 7% of the population could now vote. However, this meant that five out of six males still could not vote, so in 1867 the Second Reform Act increased the franchise again by 2.5 million. This was more than Disraeli had originally intended and meant that 16% of the population could vote. The Third Reform Act in 1884 increased the franchise again which meant that two-thirds of men in England and Wales, and 29.1% of the total population, could vote. However, there was still a very large percentage of the population who could not vote, namely women. In 1918 women were eventually given the vote.

While the franchise was steadily increasing, voting procedures remained largely unchanged until 1872 when the Ballot Act was introduced. This was intended to eliminate bribery and corruption as thousands were being spent in order to bribe voters. Secret ballots were introduced as a means to wipe this out, but corruption still occurred in some areas. The Corrupt and Illegal Practices Act in 1883 filled the loopholes in the Ballot Act by limiting election expenses. The 1911 Parliament Act introduced the payment of MPs, and so by 1911 voting procedures were similar to modern-day procedures.

Popular involvement steadily increased between 1850 and 1918. The Reform Acts enfranchised the middle classes, urban working classes and agricultural workers. The rise of the press helped develop new political ideas and new parties were formed as a result. The rise of trade unions ensured improved pay and conditions for workers. All of these factors ensured human rights would be enshrined by the law, which is a key feature of democracy. By the early 20th Century women were beginning to participate in politics and were allowed on local councils, therefore popular involvement continued to increase.

Before the Reform Acts the share of power was dominated by the landowning class, with both Houses of Parliament being controlled by property owners. The industrial revolution, however, created a new middle class, who claimed that, as they were the new wealth creators, they should have a share of the power. In 1868, measures were taken which resulted in a number of constituencies being disenfranchised. A redistribution of seats followed. The Third Reform Act pronounced that voting qualifications in towns and countries

Essay 1 continued ➤

HOW TO PASS HIGHER HISTORY

Essay 1 *continued*

should be identical. In 1885 the total number of MPs was increased to 670. Although these measures had been taken it was not until after the 1911 Parliament Act that the share of power became balanced. The Act limited the power of the House of Lords and restricted the life of a parliament to five years.

In conclusion, by 1918 Britain had made numerous progressions towards a democracy: the franchise had increased dramatically, corruption had been wiped out, involvement in politics was increasing and the balance of power was almost equal. The enfranchisement of women in 1918 led to the system becoming almost entirely democratic and not unlike the present-day system.

Commentary on Essay 1

This essay has several excellent features, but also some obvious weaknesses. Its most important strength is that the writer sticks to the question and never wanders off into irrelevance. Its biggest weakness is that it is relatively short, so the writer quite often makes points very briefly without explaining or developing them.

Structure

The essay has a reasonably good structure. In the main part of the essay, the writer deals with four issues, each of which is given a paragraph of its own. The approach within each paragraph combines some narrative of reforms in the system of electing Parliament with analysis of the effects of each reform, and this works well in showing the writer's understanding of how far these reforms made Britain more democratic.

Introduction

The essay is introduced by a well-chosen quotation from Winston Churchill, but the effect is lost to an extent as the writer does not then *use* the quotation to lead into any kind of discussion. However, the first paragraph does several things well:

- ◆ it shows a good awareness of the key features of a democracy
- ◆ it sets the historical context fairly effectively, noting that Britain was not democratic in the early nineteenth century
- ◆ it gives a brief indication of the areas in which democracy was extended during the next 80 years or so.

Evidence

While the evidence included in the essay is both accurate and relevant, it is a little short on detail or development in places. For example:

◆ in the second paragraph the writer lists the various reforms which extended the right to vote very briefly, with little development of the implications of this in terms of the kinds of people who gained the vote

◆ in the third paragraph the point about the Corrupt and Illegal Practices Act could have been expanded and explained more fully

◆ the writer could have been more specific about ways in which the Parliament Act of 1911 limited the power of the House of Lords.

It could also be argued that some additional features of a democracy, such as changes that enabled ordinary people to stand for election as Members of Parliament, are not discussed at all.

Some of the evidence is used very well to illustrate or develop good points of analysis. There are two particularly good examples of this:

◆ in the fourth paragraph, having made the point that the Reform Acts spread the vote to new classes of people, the writer then makes a good link to two other important influences on democracy – the spread of new ideas through the press and the rise of trade unions (though it would have been even better had the writer chosen to mention *which* political ideas and parties had resulted from these developments). At this point, the writer introduces two new pieces of evidence that explain the impact of these two influences – by referring to their effects on the place of human rights and on the participation of women in some aspects of politics. The use of the short phrase 'therefore popular involvement continued to increase' summarised the argument of the paragraph very effectively.

◆ in the fifth paragraph there is a basic point about the shift of power from the landowning to the middle-class. This point may be basic, but it is made very strongly by the use of two pieces of detail: the fact that the middle-class had been created by the industrial revolution and the basis of their claim to a share of power – 'as they were the new wealth creators'. Without having to say it directly, the writer shows an understanding of the nineteenth century argument, sometimes used by opponents of reform, that Parliament did not represent the people of the country but its sources of wealth. This is an excellent analytical point, made without fuss.

Conclusion

Sadly, the conclusion is not up to the quality of some of the rest of the essay. It is too short, merely listing a few changes that had taken place but without any real evaluation of how effectively these had made Britain more democratic. There is a statement to that effect in the last sentence, but it is not convincing and does not, for instance, consider ways in which it could be argued that Britain could become yet *more* democratic.

Overall

This is a very promising essay with some good features but also some disappointments. Though it shows good understanding of the main themes, and there are some quite su___ points of analysis, there is a general lack of development and a rather weak conclusion, which limit the mark to a middle B.

Essay 2

How democratic was Britain by 1918?

Democracy is not simply having the right to vote in parliamentary elections. For a country to be truly democratic other conditions must exist first. There must be a wide franchise which will allow more people to vote and will make the result more representative of people's thoughts, opinions and needs. There should also be a fair distribution of seats around the country so that all constituencies are equally represented. Voting must be free from influence, corruption and bribery so that people aren't scared to vote and the final result is true and fair. The government must also be representative of the majority vote. By 1918 Britain had developed politically and was moving toward democracy; however, some of these conditions hadn't fully been met which hindered British politics and meant that in 1918 Britain wasn't a democracy.

By 1918 the franchise had been widened and more people were allowed to vote. In 1867 Britain introduced the Second Reform Act which meant that more men could vote, and now one in three had the vote. The Second Reform Act showed Britain was widening the franchise; however, it still wasn't wide enough as more than 50% of men still couldn't vote and women could not vote at all. Whilst the Third Reform Act in 1884–85 improved on the Second Reform Act by giving more and more men the right to vote, it was still very poor. In 1918 property qualification had also been lowered because in 1858 there was the abolition of the Property Qualification. People who were educated and owned less property could now vote. By 1918 it is evident that the franchise had been widened, however many people could still not vote. Women were not allowed to vote at all and two in five men still could not vote. Historian T C Smout states: 'The Third Reform Act (1884) left some 40% of the adult males in the UK still disenfranchised in 1918.' Granted the British democratic system was improving, but it wasn't fully democratic because the huge majority of the population were still unable to vote. The 60% of males who were allowed to vote no longer had to vote in the open and were not subject to bribery and corruption by 1918. The Representation of the People Act 1918 also saw the franchise widened, allowing even more people to vote. Women over thirty were now allowed to vote.

In the early and mid-1800s corrupt elections were common: people eligible to vote were offered bribes or in some cases threatened so they would vote a certain way. The elections were held openly and everybody knew who people had voted for, which meant people were intimidated and too scared to vote. In 1872 the Secret Ballot Act was introduced. This meant people voted in private and their identity was anonymous; therefore the final result of the election was far more fair and representative. In 1883 the Corrupt and Liberal Practices Act was introduced which saw bribery and influencing elections become a criminal offence. By

Essay 2 continued ➢

Essay 2 continued

1911 the majority of people voted in secret, fair and honest conditions which contributed to Britain being far more democratic by 1918.

In the early and mid-1800s Britain's economy thrived on agriculture and land owners in the countryside were the majority of voters. When the UK became more industrialised and the source of economy was changing, politics remained the same. The seat distribution was extremely unequal and the south and south-west of England were still heavily favoured, leaving the industrial northern cities such as Leeds under-represented. In 1885 the Redistribution of Seats Act was introduced, leaving all areas fairly represented. The seats (MPs) were distributed more equally and the north started to be represented in the House of Commons. However, the agricultural areas still dominated Parliament as the majority of MPs came from rural areas. In 1918 northern seats were more common which showed an equal spread of representation was rising, however many areas were still poorly represented. Scotland only had 53 seats, proving that Britain still wasn't a democracy by 1918 but the system had improved massively.

Before 1858, to become a Member of Parliament there was a land qualification where a potential MP had to have £610 of land or £300 worth of property. This was unfair because the working class people who wanted to become MPs did not qualify if they didn't have any property or land. Even if they could barely qualify they could not afford to become MPs because at that time MPs did not get a salary, which meant they didn't get paid a wage for full-time work. The 1858 Abolition of Property Qualification made it easier for working class to break through and become Members of Parliament. In 1911 the Parliamentary Act saw a salary introduced and more regular elections from every seven years to every five years. This made it easier for working class people to become MPs as there were fewer factors to hinder their climb into Parliament. However, many still found it hard to become MPs and the House of Commons were still heavily dominated by members of the aristocracy.

Britain was not fully democratic by 1918 as women were still heavily left out of the democratic system. Whilst Britain was moving towards democracy because of the introduction of many acts widening the franchise and making a more fair and safer voting system. However, Britain still had a long way to go to become fully democratic.

Commentary on Essay 2

This essay shares some of the strengths and weaknesses of Essay 1, but is a little better in that its points are developed more fully. This essay's main strength is the way in which it considers different aspects of a democratic country and assesses what progress Britain had made in each area by 1918. Like Essay 1, there is a strong introduction but a relatively weak conclusion.

Structure

This essay has a good structure, with good use of paragraphs to organise the evidence. The approach combines description of the political changes in Britain with analysis that shows fairly convincingly that the writer understands why these had made Britain democratic by 1918 but also that there was still room for more reform.

Introduction

There is a very strong introduction, showing clearly what features the writer would expect to be present in a democracy, and indicating the likely argument in the rest of the essay, which is that some of these existed in Britain by 1918, but not all.

Evidence

There is more evidence in this essay than in Essay 1, and in general it is accurate and relevant, though there are a few minor errors which spoil the effect a little. For example, in the third paragraph the Corrupt and Illegal Practices Act is called the "Corrupt and Liberal Practices Act". Small slips like this would not, however, be penalised in the examination unless they were very common.

In places, the writer uses evidence skilfully to illustrate or develop points in the argument. Two examples will demonstrate how this is done:

◆ in the second paragraph the writer is arguing that, although the franchise had been widened by 1918, that process was not yet complete. This point is then driven home by the use of a well-chosen quotation from an historian, T.C. Smout, to highlight the specific point that the Third Reform Act left 40% of adult males without the vote. The argument is then explained neatly in the statement 'granted the British democratic system was improving. However, it wasn't fully democratic because the huge majority of the people were unable to vote'.

◆ there is a good interplay between evidence and analysis in the fifth paragraph, where the writer discusses the ability of working-class people to stand for election. After noting that working-class people could not satisfy the property qualification, the writer then makes the excellent point that 'even if they could barely qualify, they could not afford to become MPs because at the time MPs did not get a salary'. At this stage, the writer introduces two facts: that the issue of the property qualification, at least, was removed in 1858, and that the Parliament Act of 1911 introduced payment for MPs. The discussion is then concluded with a neat point of analysis emphasising that this was not a complete solution as there were still few working-class MPs.

Conclusion

While relevant, the conclusion is disappointing by comparison with the rest of the essay, like that in Essay 1. The short conclusion does offer an answer to the question, but there is only a brief discussion of the factors that led the writer to reach this answer.

Overall

This essay does have a number of weaknesses, most obviously the short conclusion. However, there are also considerable strengths in the clear introduction, good selection and use of evidence, and efforts throughout to make an argument. These strengths outweigh the weaknesses enough to mean that the essay is worth a borderline A pass.

Essay 3

Did the political opposition groups in Tsarist Russia offer any real threat to the Government before 1905?

Political opposition groups that were illegal in Russia before 1905 were: the Social Democratic Labour Party (SDLP), the Liberals and the Socialist-Revolutionary Party (SR). These parties tried to threaten the Tsar in different ways: the SDLP wanted to wait for a 'magic moment' to rise up and use force to control the state, the Liberals were peaceful and wanted a constitutional monarch and the SRs wanted to get rid of the Tsar altogether and help the peasants. Heavily oppressed and suppressed, it was not hard to see why these illegal political movements wanted rid of the Tsar and his tyrannical government.

The SDLP had two leaders: Lenin and Martov. At the London Conference of 1903 there was a big discussion on what the SDLP stood for and this led to the break-up of the SDLP. They broke off into two groups: the Bolsheviks, ruled by Lenin, and the Mensheviks who were ruled by Martov. The Bolsheviks wanted a small party whose members who were elitist-professional revolutionaries, with a large base of non-party support. They wanted rid of the Tsar completely. The Bolsheviks did not get that involved in the 1905 revolution because by the time Lenin got back into the country Nicholas II had drafted up the October Manifesto and the revolution was over. The Bolsheviks had three journals/papers, one of which was the Vpceryod (translated to English it means 'Forward'). The Mensheviks, however, had kept control of the SDLP paper known as Iskra. The Menshevik leader, Martov, believed in a state without the Tsar but the party were not as extreme and did not want what is known today as Communism. Instead the party wanted trade unions, a parliament and civil rights. They were much like the Liberals, except the Liberals did not mind the Tsar being in power. Lenin believed that they were not revolutionary and just tinkering with capitalism. The Mensheviks got their money from supporters unlike the Bolsheviks, who robbed banks. Lenin also used money he inherited from his father to fund the party. By 1914 the Bolsheviks had non-party support of 20,000 but by 1917 it had exploded to 300,000. Overall, before 1905 this group did not offer much of a threat to Tsarism because all of the Bolsheviks' leaders were in exile from the country and only a few party members were in Russia. The Mensheviks were seen by the Tsar to be too busy quarrelling with themselves and with the Bolsheviks about issues. So although the Bolsheviks went on to rule Russia, before the time of 1905 it seemed like the SDLP were not that big a threat to Tsarism. Also the Okhrana often had inside information on the SDLP.

The Liberals were also broken into two different groups: the Kadets and the Octobrists who came into play after 1905. The Kadets were a middle class group of people who wanted a lot of change to the Tsarist state. They wanted civil rights, a parliament, a constitution, freedom of speech and a voting system. Some of this they got after 1905 in the October Manifesto with the Duma being set up. The Liberals did not want the Tsar to abdicate but they wanted to move forward with the times unlike the backward-thinking Nicholas II. They would go to meeting place like bars and saloons where groups of people would debate their views. The Liberals were much more philosophical and had no real intention to change the way the Government ruled. Overall the Liberals were no threat to the rule of the Tsar

Essay 3 continued ➤

Essay 3 *continued*

because they did not want him to abdicate and had no intention of revolution. They tried not to get into wrong-doings but this was a difficult thing to do in the oppressed state of Russia. The Liberals were a threat to the way the Tsar ruled Russia because they wanted all trade unions and a constitution. The Tsar gave them this in the October Manifesto.

The final, most violent, group was the Socialist-Revolutionary Party (SR). The leader was Victor Chernov, who was part of the populists who assassinated Alexander II. Their first full conference was held in 1906 in Finland. The group was backward thinking and favoured the peasant. They wanted to solve the day-to-day problems like starvation and education. One of the bigger things they wanted rid of were the redemption payments which Alexander II had made them pay for the land they bought when they were released from serfdom. This led them to commit thousands of terrorist acts, many of which were aimed at the Ministry of the Interior and which were very successful. They disagreed with Marxists about the idea that peasants could not hold up a revolution, but agreed that the Tsar needed to go. However, what split them up was that they were backward thinking and favoured peasants, whereas the Marxists favoured the worker and wanted to create an industrial state. The SR was the biggest threat to the Tsar through assassination but were not that powerful because the Okhrana often had people working for them who kept a close eye on the SR. The army could be easily mobilised to attack any uprising.

In conclusion to this, the Tsar was only at threat if the army was fighting a war and could not be called in. The groups were not that powerful – they were still a threat but not as large as they had been made out to be. The SR posed the biggest threat.

Commentary on Essay 3

The writer of this essay has a decent knowledge of the political opposition groups in Russia, but never really focuses on the question. Most of the essay describes the various opposition groups, but there is no real discussion about how far they represented a threat to the Tsarist state.

Structure

The essay is organised appropriately into paragraphs, with each of the three main groups being given a paragraph of its own. However, the approach is almost entirely descriptive, with only a couple of points of evaluation.

Introduction

This is a pretty basic introduction, which does nothing more than list the main opposition groups and say what they wanted. The writer does not even mention the issue of how dangerous these were as a threat to the Tsarist state.

Evidence

There is a reasonable amount of information about the opposition groups, with a good amount of detail in places. All of this could be relevant to the question, but it is rarely *used* to develop any points of analysis. Only twice in the essay is there any real attempt to make a point of evaluation:

◆ towards the end of paragraph two there is a statement that the Social Democrats 'did not offer much of a threat to Tsarism', followed by two reasons: that the Bolshevik leaders were in exile and the Mensheviks were arguing among themselves. However, this point is made only briefly.

◆ near the end of paragraph three there is an even simpler point about the Liberals being no threat because they had no intention of revolution.

Another weakness in this essay is that the writer largely ignores factors other than the nature of the political parties themselves. Almost all of the discussion is about the parties individually, with little reference to the fact that disagreements between the parties weakened their position as possible dangers to the government. Furthermore, there is no mention of the methods of repression that made opposition to the Tsarist state so difficult in Russia. For these reasons, the evidence is not as strong as it should have been.

Conclusion

There is hardly any conclusion at all. There is a statement mentioning, for the first time, that the army was important in preventing a threat. Then there is a single sentence answering the question and a comment that the Social Revolutionaries were the biggest threat, but the conclusion is not coherent.

Overall

This is an essay with some potential, as the writer knows a fair amount about the subject and provides a little evaluation. However, the weak introduction and conclusion, the narrative approach and the absence of discussion of other factors mean that the essay never rises above the level of basic competence, and the best mark it could be given would be a middle C pass.

Essay 4

How important was Bismarck in the creation of a united Germany by 1871?

Bismarck was undoubtedly a vital factor in the unification of Germany. His combination of opportunism and diplomacy led Prussia to become an influential power on the European stage and was prominent in unifying Germany in 1871. However, Bismarck alone cannot be given all the credit for uniting Germany. Other factors of the economy, the army and nationalism must also be discussed in relation to the contribution to unification.

The 1862 constitutional crisis in Prussia is a prime example of Bismarck's opportunism. The King of Prussia wanted to raise taxes in order to modernise his army. He hoped that if Prussia was strong militarily she would gain more power in Europe. The Liberals in the parliament opposed this legislation and refused to submit to increased taxes. Bismarck was made Prussian chancellor in 1862. He was well aware that a strong army would increase Prussia's influence and so forced the legislation through. The 1864 Danish war arose from the Schleswig-Holstein crisis. Under the London protocol the Danish King was required to give up his claim to the duchies. In 1864 the Danes tried to incorporate Schleswig and Holstein into its government. Bismarck saw that by going to war with Denmark he could easily establish Prussia as the leader of Germany and extend Prussian territory. After making an alliance with Austria, Bismarck had shown the Liberals that the army reforms were necessary and that force was the way to achieve aims. Furthermore, on the provocation of the French war, Bismarck again illustrated his opportunism. Several minor events, such as the Luxembourg and Belgian railways fiascos, illustrated Bismarck's ability as a manipulator of his opponents' weaknesses. However, the issues of the Spanish candidature and the Ems telegram were more major factors. The Spanish parliament offered Prince Leopold of Prussia their throne. Bismarck instantly recognised how a Prussian on the Spanish throne could be seen as a threat to France and so bribed both sides to accept. The Ems telegram was a note which the King sent to Bismarck concerning the Spanish candidature. Bismarck, ever searching for ways to increase Franco-Prussian tension, edited the telegram and released it to the press. This infuriated the French and was a major factor which led to war.

However, Bismarck was not only a brilliant opportunist but a diplomat who created advantageous situations. After the Danish war, Austria and Prussia agreed to joint rule of the duchies. However, this failed and war nearly started between the two powers. Bismarck was not ready for war and so he met with Austria at the Gastein Convention. Here, Bismarck manipulated Austria into occupying Holstein whilst Prussia occupied Schleswig. This meant that the Austrian garrison was surrounded by Prussian territory, making it easy for Bismarck to provoke war when it best suited Prussia. Mitchell wrote: 'The Gastein Convention was a masterstroke.' Another example of Bismarck's diplomatic skills can be seen in the issue of French compensation. Before the Austro-Prussian War Bismarck had secured French neutrality by promising territory in the south German states. When the Austro-Prussian War was over Napoleon sought his compensation. Bismarck refused his claim saying that there was no written proof of their meeting at Biarritz. Accordingly, Napoleon put his demands in writing and Bismarck shrewdly released them to the press. This final international snub

Essay 4 continued ➤

Essay 4 continued

provoked the French into declaring war on Prussia, Bismarck's initial aim. Thomson wrote: 'The pieces on the European chessboard remained exactly as he (Bismarck) wanted them.'

The German economy was another factor which lead to unification. The formation of the Zollverein (free trade area) in Prussia encouraged Germans to see the economic benefits of unification.

The Prussian army gave Prussia the strength to fight its European wars and gradually allowed Bismarck to manipulate Germans into uniting in Germany. The Prussian army also established Prussia as the strong leader of Germany, without whom unification could never have occurred.

Finally, the force of nationalism played a part in uniting Germany. The peaceful 1848 Revolution in Germany brought the issue of nationalism to the forefront of popular debate.

In conclusion, Bismarck's opportunism and diplomatic skills were of great importance to the unification of Germany in 1871. However, other factors such as the economy, the army and nationalism must also be taken into account. Seaman: 'Bismarck had operated in what was essentially a favourable diplomatic climate.'

Commentary on Essay 4

This is an unusual essay, with some very good points as well as some real frustrations – a little more planning and some additional development could have turned it into an outstandingly good one. The writer's understanding of Bismarck's contribution to the unification of Germany is more sophisticated than examiners often see, as the approach avoids the very common one where the three wars are described in detail but with little analysis. Here, the writer discusses several aspects of Bismarck's talents: his opportunism, ability to exploit mistakes by his opponents and diplomatic skills. What prevents the essay from reaching the highest levels is that, although recognising that unification also resulted from other factors, these are mentioned only very briefly, so there is no proper comparison of their importance with that of Bismarck, as required by the question.

Structure

The structure is reasonably good, with a recognisable introduction and conclusion and with some attempt to use paragraphs, though the two long paragraphs both cover two issues instead of one. New paragraphs at 'Furthermore, on the provocation of the French war…' and 'Another example of Bismarck's diplomatic skills…' would have improved the flow of the essay. The overall approach is analytical rather than narrative. Though there are some quotations from historians, these are not chosen particularly well and they are not used very effectively, giving the impression they are there for effect rather than for a positive purpose.

Introduction

This is a standard, competent introduction that recognises what Bismarck contributed to the unification of Germany and identifies three other important factors, though very briefly.

Evidence

There are very different approaches to discussing the evidence about Bismarck and the evidence about other factors. Bismarck is treated in considerable detail, but not in the usual way. The writer uses evidence well on several occasions to illustrate useful points of analysis. For example:

◆ in the second paragraph the writer links the ideas that Bismarck was an opportunist and that he was able to manipulate his opponents' weaknesses. To show this, the writer makes a small point about minor events to lead into discussion of the Spanish candidature and the Ems telegram, which are identified as more important factors. This leads to an explanation of how these were used to provoke France into declaring war.

◆ to develop the point, at the start of the next paragraph the writer explains that Bismarck used the Convention of Gastein to create the conditions in which he could provoke war at a convenient moment.

Not all of the evidence works so well. Having stated in the second paragraph that the Ems telegram provoked France to declare war, there is some confusion in the third paragraph in the statement that it was Bismarck's publication of Napoleon III's demands at Biarritz that led to the outbreak of war.

More seriously, the writer makes only the briefest of references to the Zollverein, the importance of the Prussian army and the rise of nationalism. More exploration of these factors, cutting back on some of the discussion of Bismarck if necessary, would have given a much better balance to the essay.

Conclusion

The conclusion is much too short, effectively re-stating points from the introduction and quoting an historian without linking it to the writer's words. A conclusion such as the one on page 37 would have given the essay a much stronger climax.

Overall

This had the potential to be an outstanding essay, given the skills of analysis and use of evidence that are present, but the weaknesses outlined above would prevent the award of a mark higher than a top band B.

Chapter 9

Essay 5

Should the main credit for Red Victory in the Civil War be given to Trotsky?

The Bolsheviks came to power in 1917 and faced a few problems and quite a lot of opposition but by 1921, after a three-year civil war, they were in power and running the state under capitalism. How had this been achieved? Was it all due to Trotsky? By examining the Reds and the Whites separately we will determine if this is the case.

Firstly, it must be said that the Bolsheviks' main tool during the war was Trotsky – he was indispensable and Lenin set him in charge of building a Red Army. Trotsky created it with the 1000 Red Guards who had helped with the revolution, or the 'nucleus', as McColgan refers to them, plus Latvian rifle divisions and Baltic sailors. In March 1919 the Red Army equalled 500,000 but by June 1920, after conscription had been implemented, there were over 5 million troops. Of these 5 million, 75,000 were women who were allowed to fight on every front, with every weapon, and took 1800 casualties. Even though they totalled 5 million, only about 10% were used for fighting. The Red Army was trained: some highly effective, others 'little better than a rabble' (McColgan). In addition to this mighty display of troops, which was the biggest at this time, was Trotsky's leadership. He was considered to be a great leader because he could instil a new fighting spirit in the troops wherever they were. He also promoted soldiers who showed courage or initiative and killed those who betrayed him. By decimation he put fear into the soldiers which made them obey and in the case of the old Tsarist officers brought into the Red Army, their families were threatened to make sure they never betrayed. Trotsky also had his armoured train which was full of propaganda and good food. This is why in some case Trotsky was seen to be indispensable.

Other factors also have to be accounted for when questioning the Reds' victory. Other topics were economic and social factors. The Reds controlled the internal railway lines around the city and were able to move troops and supplies quickly. Due to this the Reds preferred to fight at railway heads. The propaganda used by the Reds was also highly effective as it portrayed the Whites as being in favour of the land being given back to the Lords. This made the peasants, who had never favoured anybody, prefer the Reds. This gradually changed when the Bolsheviks announced their use of war-communism to help them win the war. It was also passed due to the fact that over a course of nine years, Russia had lost 28 million people. Five of those years were under the Bolsheviks. This policy of war-communism allowed them to have more control of public life and collect grain for the soldiers. This caused upset for the peasants when told any extra was being collected and to combat this the peasants grew only enough for themselves. 1920 saw various uprisings by peasants. The Cheka were called in to help the Bolsheviks and if they found anyone secreting food they shot them. As we can see from the Reds point of view, everything was going their way and Trotsky was a major part. The peasants weren't necessarily with the Reds but they didn't have to be – the Cheka could sort them out.

Another reason for the Red victory in the Russian Civil War was the basic lack of good Generals for the Whites. The Whites consisted of Cadets who didn't like the new regime,

HOW TO PASS HIGHER HISTORY

Essay 5 continued ➤

Essay 5 *continued*

church-goers who passionately hated what the Bolsheviks stood for, and landlords and factory owners who wanted their land and factories returned to them. The three main White leaders were Admiral Kolchack, General Denikin and General Yudenich. Kolchack, from the east, travelled along the Trans-Siberian railway and posed the first major threat to the Reds. He also had 100,000 Japanese men, 150,000 arms from the US, and British tanks, but 150,000 men still had no effect against the 100,000 men of the Reds who defeated the Whites. General Denikin, on the other hand, was from the south and had captured the main supply line of the Reds. Again, however, Trotsky instilled a new spirit in his troops and they defeated the Whites. Finally, there was General Yudenich who came from the west and attempted to capture the Reds twice but was again forced to retreat. Other reasons why they had to retreat were the bad behaviour of the White Troops and the corrupt administrative services they held. This shows yet another reason why the Whites failed and the Reds succeeded.

The final reason for the failure of the Whites was the basic lack of co-ordination and future plans – all denounced Bolshevism but announced nothing. Each of the three Generals worked separately and were often in competition. Foreign intervention never helped much as the Bolsheviks could use it to their advantage and claim that these three leaders were pawns in Western imperialism.

By this look at both the Whites and Reds, there are many reasons as to why the Reds won. Trotksy is the most prominent but the economic and social advantages – or 'material advantages' as Pipes calls them – shouldn't be forgotten. Even more important are the weaknesses of the Whites, of which there are several. Only if these three Generals had worked together and hadn't been misled by the intervention of foreign nations could we perhaps see a different story.

Commentary on Essay 5

Here is another essay with strengths and weaknesses. There is analysis in places, but not consistently throughout the essay, as some sections become heavily narrative. This time, the conclusion is stronger than the introduction.

Structure

The approach is generally thematic. The writer considers several factors affecting the outcome of the Civil War – Trotsky first (probably because this is the 'isolated factor' mentioned in the question), followed by economic and social factors and then the weaknesses of the White generals and their forces. Within each of these themes there is a mixture of narrative and analysis, with some good use of evidence in places to develop points, though in other areas the evaluations are a little simple.

Though the writer uses paragraphs to divide points, the argument might have been helped by breaking up a couple of very long paragraphs. For example, a break after the quote from McColgan in the second paragraph would have shown that the discussion is now of a different point – Trotsky's leadership rather than the Red Army itself.

Introduction

This is an acceptable, if basic, introduction that refers to the wording of the question and sets the issue in context, albeit very briefly. There is a slip of the pen, where 'capitalism' should read 'communism', but this is the kind of accident that can happen under pressure and examiners would not treat it severely.

Evidence

There is a good volume of evidence, though some factors are omitted, most importantly the fact that the Bolshevik control of the central part of Russia allowed better coordination and control of their military efforts. *Some* of the evidence is used well to develop points of analysis. In the second paragraph, for instance, the writer makes the valid point that Trotsky instilled a new fighting spirit in the troops of the Red Army and then uses specific pieces of evidence to explain how this was done: promoting soldiers who showed courage or initiative; using decimation to force obedience through fear; pressurising former Tsarist officers by holding their families hostage and the use of the armoured train and propaganda.

Unfortunately, this use of evidence is not consistent throughout the essay:

◆ the section dealing with the three main White armies is largely narrative, listing rather than explaining the defeats of these armies.

◆ the writer says that Kolchak (whose name is mis-spelled) had men and weapons from Japan, the USA and Britain, 'but the 150,000 men still had no effect against the 100,000 men of the Reds who defeated the Whites'. But there is no explanation of why this apparently superior army lost.

◆ the writer gives only the briefest of explanations for the defeats of Denikin and Yudenich. More analysis of the varying reasons for Red victory in these campaigns would have been welcome.

There are a few useful references to historians, though they are used to reinforce points of fact rather than indicating any historical debate. There is also occasional vagueness, such as early in paragraph four, where the description of which groups made up the Whites could have been more precise.

Conclusion

Although the conclusion could have considered the arguments in favour of Trotsky at greater length, there is still a serious attempt to balance the influence of the various factors. Of these five essays, this is the best conclusion.

Overall

This is an essay of much promise, but it fails to deliver in a number of ways. The qualities of knowledge and of analysis, together with a fairly strong conclusion, mean that it is a good pass, but the flaws outlined about would make the essay worth a middle B rather than the A pass that could have been achieved through better organisation of the evidence.